A WOMAN'S PLACE IS
in the cockpit!

a memoir

BETH NIEBUHR

Contents

Chapter 1

Highlights

"What if he won't let go?" I worried again and again. This fear didn't just preoccupy my thoughts during daylight hours; it even invaded my sometimes not-so-restful nights.

As an average-size woman, 5'5" and 125 pounds, I would be unlikely to overpower even a below-average-size man. Of course, this is true of most women, but I had a special reason for my obsession: in just a few days, I would be starting my new job as a flight instructor.

I had spent hundreds of flight hours and thousands of study hours in preparation for this exciting time. I was very eager to share my joy of flying with all the students I could coax into choosing me as their mentor.

However, I did have two major concerns: how to know when a would-be pilot is ready for the first solo, and the possibility that a frightened but determined pupil would not allow me to rescue us from his mistake.

The available textbooks were not very chatty. The sections on when to solo a student were about regulations and did not take into consideration individual personalities. However, I plunged ahead, hoping that I would assess correctly when the time came. And I did.

But as to the other concern, it was never mentioned in anything I read, even though I devoured every word on instructing that I could find. My role models were strong men; they didn't have this concern, and I didn't ask them.

As it turned out, my worries were for nothing. I soon learned that my attitude was what was important. I was totally comfortable in a plane, and it showed. The student took his cues from me. Learning to fly should be fun. And, if things went wrong, I could fix it.

This trust building started from day one of the fledgling's flying experience. The little Cessna airplane moved jerkily through the air, maneuvered by the hesitant student pilot. Obediently, it responded to the movements of his limbs, lurching as his foot jabbed a rudder pedal, skidding as his hands clumsily directed the wings. Then I would demonstrate the correct input, and the little plane responded gracefully.

After I became a chief flight instructor and conducted stage checks with other people's students, I had to use different tactics. I recall one nice middle-aged man in particular. I'll call him Nick. He had logged many hours with his instructor, but he wasn't a natural; most people beyond their twenties aren't. I asked him to show me a full stall. He began the procedure: power off, raise the nose, hold the back pressure, keep going straight with the rudder pedals, wait for the stall followed by the nose dropping, and recover by releasing the back pressure, adding full power and keep going straight with rudder use.

It's a lot to remember, but it has to become automatic. Only birds respond by instinct; for people, we emphasize the procedure to the point that it becomes a reflex.

However, Nick was so tense that he couldn't interpret the airplane's need for rudder coordination, and he probably lost his reference point outside. As the plane shuddered, he stiffened. Rather than releasing the back pressure which had initiated the stall, he held on hard and paid no attention to the pedals.

I'm sure he didn't do this with his regular teacher, but this was a stage check, and he was nervous. The outcome of this flight would determine whether he was ready to move on to the next phase—whether he was safe to fly solo. Nervousness in a novice leads to rote performance with little if any "feel" involved. And so the plane began to spin, and he looked at me in terror.

Then I laughed.

Sounds cruel, doesn't it? But he relaxed his grip slightly. I continued smiling as I told him that he needed to let go if he wanted me to save our lives. And he did.

It may have been overly dramatic, but it got his attention and he complied.

Stall practice is conducted several thousand feet about the ground. This allows for plenty of altitude with which to recover, especially for the novice. With ample room, instructors can usually talk the student through the recovery. That's better than taking over, unless the student is frozen, like Nick was on this occasion.

In fact, when I'd show a student a stall for the first time, I let the airplane recover. I always planned to do this early in a student's training, maybe in the first lesson. Often, the prospective pilot has learned from his pilot friend, who is macho indeed, that stalls are to be endured, certainly not enjoyed. We needed to get past that. I'd quickly set up a simple power-off stall, and then let go.

Sure enough, the plane wants to fly. It noses forward, picks up speed, and soon is flying again. Then I'd quickly set up another one, mentioning that this time we wouldn't lose altitude. I'd stall the plane and then recover by releasing a little back pressure and adding full power.

Why quickly? At this point, the brave pilot friend has ensured that my student is afraid of stalls, and if I don't move quickly, he will be feeling queasy pretty soon. So we move right on to a simple maneuver that he can perform by himself, and 19 times out of 20, when we have landed, he will tell me that he was surprised at how easy and safe it was. That's good enough for a few lessons; we'll get back to perfecting stalls later.

Once, after I watched a student's preflight of the airplane as part of his stage check, I told him just what we would be doing during the flight. I added that if at any time I announced, "My airplane," that he would, of course, relinquish the controls. "Mark" looked at me and said he'd have to think about that.

I told him to tie down the airplane—we were finished for now. No flying today.

I spoke to his flight instructor, who had been trained elsewhere and had only recently joined the staff. His company standardization flight apparently hadn't covered this topic. He quickly recognized the wisdom of making sure a student knew who was boss in the airplane, and Mark eventually went on to become an accomplished pilot.

Chapter 2

The Joy of Learning to Fly

I didn't know that I wanted to fly until I was 31. Unlike many pilots who dreamed about it all through their childhoods, I didn't give the possibility a thought. I was a girl; as most girls didn't consider piloting an option, I didn't think about it at all. One clue might have been that, earlier, when it was time to get a tyke bike for my tiny daughter, I chose a tyke airplane for her.

One funny thing: at the first college I attended, a small school in Kansas, the rules for girls were quite strict. We had "hours," which meant that we had to be in our rooms by a certain time each night. Also, our parents had to fill out a questionnaire specifying what extracurricular activities we were allowed to engage in: visits away from school on weekends, going on other types of trips, and so forth.

The only activity my parents disallowed was going on an airplane flight. Although later, when I became a pilot, they enjoyed taking little flights with me in my small airplane.

I was never in an airplane until I was 27. When it finally happened, I immediately loved it, especially the rush of the takeoff. But I still didn't think of piloting myself. I simply started planning subsequent trips to favor flights with as many legs as possible, so that there would be more takeoffs.

I didn't learn that I was born to fly until a flight when I was 31. My husband and I were invited to share a flight in a Cessna 205 with two other couples for a weekend trip: George, the pilot, and Sally; Bill and Doris; Bob and me.

George was a little worried about me because I was the only one who had never been in a small plane. He suggested that he take me for a little sample jaunt in a Cessna 172. I thought that would be a fun because he said I could take my two young children along. Unfortunately, on the day of the proposed flight, one of my kids had a cold. A call to the pediatrician confirmed my fear that it wouldn't be a good idea to take a congested child flying.

There wasn't an opportunity to try another time before our excursion. Not a problem; I fell in love as soon as we took off! The airplane had six seats and my friend Doris and I were assigned the two smallest seats, in the back. George kept asking, "Everyone ok?" and looking back at me, checking to see if I might be turning green.

I enjoyed every minute of our flight from Santa Barbara to Mendocino and every second of our return trip, during which we flew as low as allowed over a sunny San Francisco, where I had lived for ten years. It was fascinating to see all the familiar landmarks from a few thousand feet above.

We went into the clouds as we headed back to Santa Barbara. Fortunately, George was a skilled and current instrument-rated pilot. That made the encounter with the weather an interesting development, rather than a reason to land short of our destination at another airport.

I can't explain what it was, although the acceleration before takeoff, the miracle of liftoff, and the excitement of seeing my world from above were factors. But I was hooked! I decided then that when my younger child went to kindergarten, I would learn to fly.

And I did.

~~~~~~~~~~~~~~

I wasn't sure how to go about learning to fly. I did know one flight instructor, a casual friend, so I asked him. He was a good source because he taught a ground school for private pilots. He recommended the class, which was offered at Santa Barbara City College. I attended that, and he also directed me to one of the two local flight schools where he had instructing privileges. He took me on an intro, which is a short, inexpensive flight designed to show how easy it is to fly and to enthuse the prospect. To say the least, I was very enthused!

I couldn't take lessons from this friend because he had a real job as a physics college professor and didn't have time for regular students. As I learned later, it isn't a good idea to learn from a very part-time instructor anyway. You really need someone who is immersed in the airport culture and is there full-time. These are the instructors who know all the latest developments—changes in regulations, familiarity with the airplanes and their maintenance, easy access to training aids, etc.

People think they want to take lessons from the most experienced pilots on the block, preferably a 747 captain. In reality, even if one were willing to do it, he'd not likely be the best teacher. It would have been so many years ago that he trained a private pilot, he probably wouldn't do a good job.

I earned my degree in music (piano), and I gave piano lessons while I was in college. I don't do that anymore, and I know I wouldn't be a good piano teacher now. That's why I never acquiesce to a request that I teach someone to play. Also, like the 747 captain, I really don't want to.

Since my friend wasn't available to teach me, he asked the chief pilot at the school to recommend an instructor for me. He did, and I signed up.

My first flight instructor was "Irv." The first lesson with him was exciting; we actually landed at the closest airport, in Santa Ynez, and I called a friend to say, "Guess where I am!"

Learning to fly was the most exhilarating project I ever attempted. It was also the most frustrating. There are hundreds of things to learn, and since they are interrelated, many need to be learned at once. I found that to be nearly impossible. I can only learn one thing at a time.

Fortunately, there are some things that can be done sequentially. Following a checklist, for example, allows the budding pilot to proceed from one item to another. There are lots of checklists: before starting the engine, starting the engine, shutting down, and others.

Emergency checklists can also be followed step by step, but you need to know them perfectly. If your engine stops, you'd better know to lower the nose before you reach for the list, or you'll lose airspeed and find yourself in a stall. This may result in more altitude lost than you can afford. Usually, it is possible to restart the engine by trying each of the items on the checklist, but in the worst case, you would need to make an emergency landing, very likely not at an airport. You can buy time by flying at the best glide speed—the speed that gives you the most range. Sometimes that extra time is critical in finding a decent place to land.

It doesn't take too long before the basics (straight and level, turns, climbs and ascents) become familiar. Then they can be combined into climbing and descending turns. As your knowledge builds, you can work on changes of airspeed while maintaining level flight, or changing airspeed at a constant rate of climb or descent. That will lead into slow flight, stalls, and ground reference maneuvers. All of these eventually form the components of the trickiest maneuver: the landing.

I loved learning how to make the little plane follow my directions. I became familiar with commanding my hands and feet (not verbally, of course) and receiving input from them. I memorized the steps. I practiced them in my head. And then I got to actually cause a real airplane to do my bidding.

At first, it was very tiring, but soon I learned to let the airplane do the bulk of the work by means of a neat technique called trimming. I would set up the attitude, which is the picture that I could see through the windscreen. For maintaining a climb, descent, or level flight, I learned to match the horizon with an imaginary spot on windscreen that would produce the result I wanted. I would move the nose of the plane up or down to set the appropriate pitch. Counterintuitively, this is achieved by moving the tail up and down using the horizontal stabilizer. Then I would set the power to allow the speed I needed. Fortunately, this part was easy—you push the power control forward for more speed or pull it back for less.

Then the magic: the trim wheel is rolled forward or backward until it doesn't require any control pressure from the hands of the pilot (well, okay, the student pilot) to keep the plane moving along as ordered—by me!

To keep the plane going straight, I could look at a point far away in the direction I wanted to fly and just steer toward it using the ailerons and the rudder. You move the ailerons by turning the yoke, which is similar to a car's steering wheel. You control the rudder by operating pedals with your feet. It takes a while to learn how to use them together smoothly so that your eventual passengers won't even know that they are experiencing a gentle bank. An experienced pilot achieves this coordination by feel, not even having to think about it. This skill is nicknamed "flying by the seat if your pants," and new student pilots take time to develop the skill and become sufficiently relaxed to be able to achieve it.

All of my lessons were fascinating. I wasn't afraid. I longed for the day when I would fly my first solo flight.

In my car, on the way to and from the airport, I would look at car licenses and practice the aviation phonetic alphabet—Alpha, Bravo, Charlie, Delta, and so forth—by reading the letters from the licenses and converting them: 23TFA would be 23 Tango, Foxtrot, Alpha.

When communicating with a control tower, a pilot identifies the plane by its "tail number," a unique alphanumeric string of four to six letters and numbers, usually located on the tail of the plane. This number is also called the N number because aircraft registered in the USA all have the letter N at the beginning of the string. Generally, when flying in the US, the N is omitted from communications, because it is assumed. Later, when I flew into Mexico, I would include the N because Mexican plane numbers start with XA, XB, or XC.

Along the way, I learned to communicate with Santa Barbara Tower. Aviation-speak seems like a foreign language at first. The controllers usually have very nice voices and talk at a reasonable pace, but it often sounds like gibberish to the novice flyer.

The first time I had been told to contact "Ground point seven," I wondered aloud what that meant! Later, I understood, switched my communications radio to frequency 121.7, and requested and received taxi directions. Almost all airports use 121-point-something for a ground control frequency.

My friend Jan told me that one time when she called the tower for a return to the airport after a solo flight in the practice area, she was told to report "Two Guys." She said she told the controller that she had enough trouble seeing the airplanes, let alone observing who was in them. Yes, she was familiar with the store called Two Guys; she just wasn't thinking about objects on the ground. The controller was asking her to tell him when she was flying over this store, which was about two miles from the airport.

To give me a head start in understanding what was going on, I discovered the trick of turning on the radio to Ground Control and just listening before my instructor would join me in the airplane for the flight. That way, I could hear what the controller told the other pilots. It gave me an opportunity to write down his comments on the sky conditions, wind direction and velocity, and so forth. I knew that I'd soon have to digest the weather and airport conditions he supplied and reply to his directions.

This was before Santa Barbara Airport's air traffic control tower began airing the Airport Terminal Information Service (ATIS). The ATIS is a repeating recording of weather conditions, available on an aviation radio or by telephone. Later, as a flight instructor, I wrote out a format for my students to follow, describing the importance of these communications and letting them know what to expect. I even gave them a "cheat sheet'" to fill in as they listened to the ATIS. Other instructors asked to use my "cheat sheets" and later, when I ran the flight department, they became a standard handout.

As I learned with the weather reports, it's good to know what to expect. Knowing what will probably be said, and in what order, helps a lot. There are so many things to think about all at once while flying.

And then it happened. After accomplishing a few sloppy landings with my instructor, and thereafter many successful ones, I was released!

"Taxi to the tower," he instructed me.

I realized what was about to happen and asked Ground Control for clearance to the tower. Once there, my instructor opened the door, got out, shut the door, and walked away to the entrance of the tower where he would observe my first solo flight.

A few minutes later, I performed my usual routine: ask Ground Control for taxi to the runway, then perform a run-up: set the power to a specific rpm setting, hold the brakes harder, check the carburetor heat, check the magnetos, power back to idle. After that, I was ready.

My first solo!

"Santa Barbara Tower, Cherokee 214 Whiskey Yankee is ready for takeoff to stay in the pattern for touch and goes."

"Cherokee 4 Whiskey Yankee, Santa Barbara Tower, cleared for takeoff. Make left traffic." (The tower abbreviated the tail number of my plane to 4 Whiskey Yankee for convenience. Left traffic meant that the turns I would make in the traffic pattern would be to the left. The traffic pattern is a rectangle, of which the runway is one side.)

I took off, my heart pounding. I climbed to altitude and realized how much better the plane performed without the 200-pound flight instructor on board.

I reached pattern altitude quickly, leveled off, turned (to the left) downwind, and called, "Santa Barbara Tower, 4 Whiskey Yankee is downwind."

"4 Whiskey Yankee, Santa Barbara Tower, cleared for touch and go."

Oh boy! My first solo landing! Or should I say my first AT-TEMPT at a solo landing...

I went through all the procedures: power reduction, check carburetor heat, add flaps, adjust power, trim after each step, power off, and, "chirp, chirp," the noise of the tires announcing a nice landing.

I cleaned up the airplane: flaps off, roll the trim wheel a couple times, and then took off again and repeated the procedure. After my third takeoff, I began to comprehend the enormity of what was happening and my mind raced. "What am I doing up here? What if I can't do it again?"

Nevertheless, I continued. Well, what choice was there? You can't just decide that enough is enough; there's still the earth to re-encounter before quitting for the day. So, as I had been coached, I asked the tower for a full stop to conclude my flight of three takeoffs and landings, and heard, "4 Whiskey Yankee, Santa Barbara Tower, cleared to land."

Once more, I successfully encountered the runway. I allowed my-self a sigh of relief. Then, as I rolled down the strip, I heard the friendly voice of the tower controller say, "Congratulations! Turn left and con-tact Ground point seven."

"Santa Barbara Ground, Cherokee 214 Whiskey Yankee is clear of 15; taxi to the tower."

"Cherokee 4 Whiskey Yankee, Santa Barbara Ground, good job! Cross 25 and 15, and taxi to the base of the tower. When you get there, push the button next to the door and pick up the phone."

Which I did. I shut down the plane and slid across the right seat, only to realize that I didn't know how to open the door!

The pilot sits in the left seat. The right seat is for passengers, ex-cept when the real pilot-in-command (the flight instructor) occupies it. Consequently, in a plane with only one door, such as the type of Piper plane I flew, the instructor opens and closes the door.

There are two gadgets that secure the door, and I hadn't paid at-tention to the process. Another lesson to learn! Fortunately, I figured it out.

I chocked the plane, which is done by placing blocks or wedges in front of and behind at least one wheel, and headed for the door. The voice on the phone told me to take the elevator to the fourth floor. He buzzed me in.

When the elevator stopped, my instructor greeted me from a cou-ple of floors above, and I finished my climb to the top of the tower on foot. Several people were there. They all congratulated me and then looked expectantly at my instructor, who whipped out a pair of scissors and cut off my shirttail. He wrote my name, first solo, and the date on it. Next, Bob Harrison, my tower controller that day, announced that each time I soloed, I must wear that yellow shirt. After each flight, I would taxi to the tower and get another piece cut off my shirt. Ho, ho.

This was a very exciting day. I felt happy, exhilarated, proud, and best of all, part of the airport community.

I had worked hard to achieve the goal of soloing. Learning to fly is relatively easy for the average 17- to 25-year-old. They are accustomed to being in a student situation, and generally, they haven't yet coped with the concept of their own mortality. I learned at 33, a more difficult age for learning to fly, so I felt I had to try harder.

~~~~~~~~~~~~~

My training continued. It alternated between dual (with a flight instructor) and solo (just me in the plane) flights. I learned how to land in various types of fields and in windy conditions. I prepared for solo cross-country flights. I spent hours reading about how to plan them, as well as discussing my plans with instructors. I flew with them on a few dual cross-countries.

My dual cross-country flights included short flights to airports within 100 miles. Some, such as Santa Barbara to San Luis Obispo or Oxnard, featured destinations with airports much like Santa Barbara's. Other trips involved more challenging airports.

Particularly interesting were jaunts into the busy Los Angeles area. I also got to experience an airport where nobody was there (not one human being!), one with a sloping runway, and even going to one in Watsonville where there was a fly-in in progress. That one was tricky: many airplanes arriving at an airport during a short period of time and being controlled by a temporary tower, a portable setup. I'll talk more about fly-ins later.

I did more dual cross-countries than usual, not because I was a slow learner but because I wanted to know that I could handle all types of airports.

The day of my first solo cross-country, I was nervous and excited. I was well prepared, and the session with an instructor to go over my planning went well. I received the necessary signoff in my logbook and performed my preflight. I started Cherokee 15670, got clearance to the active runway, and after doing a run-up, asked for and received clearance to depart. I took off, asked the tower for a turn toward Santa Maria, and off I went.

Soon, my nervousness dissolved and I thought, "Oh, yeah, this is why I'm learning to fly—not just so that I can fly around the pattern with a teacher who constantly reminds me, 'more right rudder.' I'm going on a real trip!"

It was a great feeling! Here I was in this little airplane, which had become familiar to me in the preceding months. Instead of being a person who looked up longingly at the sight of a small plane flying above me, I was the person doing the flying.

I had become comfortable with the sounds the little craft made. The engine was very loud during takeoff and climb, it purred more quietly during the cruise, and it became increasingly quiet during a descent, with each power reduction. I didn't even need to consult the RPM gauge as I made adjustments, although I always checked it after each adjustment to confirm my accuracy.

On this day, the sky was very clear. I could see for many miles in all directions. The air was stable, and the ride was smooth. Every once in awhile, I would glance at the various gauges on the instrument panel in front of me. They verified that all was well. I felt exhilarated; I was in total control of an airplane and on my way to another airport. The view was stunning; blue sky over vibrant green vegetation nourished by recent spring rains.

I said goodbye to Santa Barbara Tower: "Request frequency change."

"Frequency change approved. Good day." The oddly old-fashioned phrase "good day" is often uttered by an air traffic controller when ceasing contact with a plane.

All of my planning worked out very well, and I made notes of my time between the checkpoints that I had selected. I calculated my groundspeed and made sure that my fuel consumption was as planned. If I had encountered unforeseen headwinds, more fuel would be required. Although I always flew with plenty of fuel, I felt that this was good training.

Also, for the first time, I actually experienced "seat of the pants" need for rudder use. The rudder allows you to feel comfortable while riding in a plane. Applying just the right amount of pressure to a rudder pedal is called coordinating the turn. Then you don't feel pushed to the side in a turn, like you sometimes do in a car. When I experienced that, it increased my elation and confidence.

The flight went smoothly. In fact, it was better than that. It made me feel secure and serene, up there in the sky by myself, and also very alert, seeing and hearing everything around me with enhanced senses.

I climbed to my cruise altitude and found all my checkpoints. They were all very close. It was only 50 miles, so it didn't take long.

I landed at the Santa Maria airport without a hitch. Of course, I had been there before, so I was confident of finding the airport. The next trips were going to be more challenging because they were new to me.

Instructors tell their cross-country students that they must have someone at the destination airport sign their logbooks. So, I proudly approached someone who worked at the airport and obtained the signature—proof of my achievement.

We students assumed that the signature was an FAA requirement. It isn't, but it tends to verify that the student did actually complete the cross-country leg. (I never heard of anyone flying in circles and forging a scribbled name, but I suppose it could happen.)

Later, when I was instructing, I realized that another benefit of this task was that it gave fledglings an extra human contact in an unfamiliar location, adding to the enjoyment of the experience. It's an awesome adventure, and some students, especially those from out of the area or from another country, do a little souvenir gathering at their destination airports.

Oh yes, there are shopping opportunities at most general aviation airports. Beyond the magazines, books, meals, and such that can be found at airline terminals, FBOs (Fixed Base Operators) and pilot supply shops offer treasures to pilots or friends who want to shop for a gift for their favorite aviators. Yes, there are books and magazines about flying—textbooks, biographies, aviation fiction, etc.—but there are also airplane Christmas ornaments, big clunky pilot watches, flight jackets, t-shirts, cute aviator bears, and many other things you don't need but may want to buy anyway. (If you really needed them, the school where you are learning to fly would probably stock them.)

The flight back to Santa Barbara was even better. I had no worries about finding the airport; all I really needed to do was head for the pass in the mountains north of Santa Barbara. It was such a beautiful day that I could see Gaviota Pass shortly after I launched. Nevertheless, I performed all the navigation tasks that I had planned. This time, though, I spent more time admiring the views, appreciating the fact that I was high above all the tiny houses, trees, and cars below me, temporarily oblivious of any cares or annoyances.

~~~~~~~~~~~~~~

It took nearly a month to complete my solo cross-country requirements. The weather just wasn't on my side. I kept rescheduling and coordinating airplane availability with my free time, as well as reserving an hour or two with an instructor to approve my plans.

My frustration over all of this got to be a joke at the flight school. People would reschedule their own cross-country flights if they spotted mine on the day they had chosen, because they feared that my bad luck would affect their flights. Really. It happened a couple of times.

Finally, on the Saturday when I was again scheduled for my long solo cross-country (x-c), I woke up to clear skies. Completing this flight would fulfill my last solo x-c requirement.

When telephoning Flight Service early in the morning, I discovered that my voice croaked a bit. My throat felt froggy, as well. Otherwise, I felt fine, so I deemed myself fit for flight. My husband and I were invited to a dinner party that evening, and I rationalized that doing a solo flight would save my voice for the festivities.

By the time my children were ready for breakfast, I had completed my flight plan except for obtaining a final weather check and the blessing of a flight instructor. After making sure that Greg and Christa's activities were planned, I went to the airport.

The instructor who cleared my flight knew that my plan had been checked by other instructors a few times before being postponed, so he just checked my weather calculations and signed my logbook. After filing the flight plan and preflighting Cherokee 15637, I was on my way to Porterville and Paso Robles.

The weather was legally adequate. For VFR, or visual flight rules, the visibility must be at least three miles. That may sound pretty good, but being able to see only three miles can actually seem to be pretty murky. In better visual conditions, a person can view a lot of landmarks: mountains, water bodies, towns, and roads, for example. Three miles' visibility reveals objects only within that relatively narrow range.

This made me nervous. Instead of feeling confident that my position was correct, I kept wondering if I was exactly where I should be. I was bothered that I couldn't see my next landmark until I was close to it.

As a pilot, when the visibility allows you to see all the landmarks shown on the sectional (a relief map issued twice a year for aviation use in a particular area), you feel confident that you are progressing accurately. Being able to see only a few miles away is a bit claustrophobic. You just wish you could verify that the town 7 miles to your left or the landing strip 15 miles on the right is really there.

During my flight, it never got worse than 3 miles visibility. Occasionally, it was more like five miles. I learned that a really clear day provides a lot more visual information and is more comfortable in which to fly. Other planes are easier to see, and having the destination in sight occurs much sooner.

I pressed on. I didn't try to save my croaky voice; I made frequent radio calls to back up my observations through the hazy sky. I chatted with Flight Service several times, asking for weather updates and making reports on my impressions of the conditions. I thought to myself that my amateur reports would be coming from the least experienced person in the air, but I complied with their requests for this information. Having taken lessons at a fairly busy airport where communicating with air traffic control had become routine, I was comfortable talking to contacts on the ground.

Air traffic controllers, flight service station personnel, and other people manning ground stations for communications tend to automatically use the pilot's voice to gauge his or her capability. That's a reasonable rule of thumb, bit it's not always accurate. A licensed pilot who always flies to and from airports with no control tower may sound inexperienced, while an avid student pilot who has studied the rules and practiced them at a controlled airport (that is, one with a control tower) will likely sound confident and able. Since I fell into the latter category, the Flight Service men that I was chatting with probably thought I was a seasoned pilot.

As I got closer to Porterville, an uncontrolled (by air traffic control) airport, I checked with Unicom. Unicom is a radio frequency that allows pilots to receive airport advisories, including the barometric pressure, wind conditions, and local traffic pattern in use for the current flight conditions. I also listened to other pilots in the area making comments and position reports.

The Porterville airport is tricky to spot on a clear day and even harder on a fuzzy one, so I used my backup plan. I flew to the VOR, a ground-based navigation transmitter located north of the city, and then back south on the radial (which gives heading guidance) along which the airport resides. Going that way, I could see a little better, and I spotted the airport in plenty of time to set up the prescribed pattern for landing. On the ground, I tied down my plane and headed for the office, where I ordered fuel and got my logbook signed.

It was an interesting day at Porterville Airport. Several hot air balloons were being staged for takeoff, and the folks manning them were friendly. One woman suggested that I stay so I could watch the flights, join the party afterwards, and stay overnight at her home. I was greatly tempted; it sounded like fun. I even called flight service to check the weather outlook for the next day. However, the weather wasn't slated to improve, and I'd have to find an instructor to sign me off tomorrow. There was also the party at home that I needed to attend.

In the end, I didn't stay very long. I also didn't go to Paso Robles. The sky condition along that route, to the west, was reported to be no better than for the leg I'd just flown. Meanwhile, I had learned that it was a bit clearer heading south. The route to Ventura promised to be pretty good, better than heading for Santa Barbara. So I changed my flight plan and went there, thinking that if I couldn't proceed to my home base, at least I would be close enough to find my way home by ground transportation or take a commercial flight if the timing was right.

I hadn't planned to go to Oxnard, where the Ventura County Airport is located, although I had been there before. The tower surprised me by greeting me with a clearance to land straight in.

Because I was flying straight toward the runway in use, not arriving from the west as I had on earlier flights, landing straight in it would be the most expeditious method and one enjoyed by experienced pilots. But I was a neophyte and felt that I couldn't judge the approach adequately. Later on in my training, I became skilled at the straight-in approach. It's fairly simple: you pick a spot on the runway and watch it. If the spot moves higher on the windscreen, you will undershoot; if it moves lower, you will overshoot. You just make corrections accordingly. But on this day, I didn't have that degree of confidence.

The usual approach to an airport involves flying three legs: downwind, base, and final. These three legs form three sides of a rectangle, allowing a pilot to check the need for altitude adjustments all along this pattern. I was used to doing it that way, so I asked for a downwind approach. With a little disdain in his voice, the controller allowed this.

I was a bit embarrassed but followed my inclination to take the easy route, even though it would take more time. Years later, I realized that the actions of the controller were more a compliment than an insult. I must have sounded competent. An obviously unskilled student pilot visiting a new airport gets hand-holding treatment to make sure he or she doesn't make a bad mistake.

After landing, I hunted down a local flight instructor. I was used to dealing with good ones, and I assumed they were all of a standard, or I would have called one I knew in Santa Barbara for advice. Instead, the local guy told me that if I just flew up the coast at 800 feet, I would be fine.

That's what I did. It was not a good idea for a student pilot, but luckily, the weather didn't deteriorate further, and it worked. Needless to say, once I became a flight instructor, I educated my students on what to do if a change of plans was necessary: call me!

I just barely got home in time to make it to the dinner party. I was eager to share the details of my adventure. That's when I discovered that many men have at least entertained the notion of flying. They are enthusiastic audiences, while their wives resist talk of such undertakings. The last thing they want for their mates is encouragement of their dreams of the skies. Either the men have already tried a flying lesson or two, or they have confided their interest in doing so. Most wives see this possibility as dangerous, expensive, and, at least, time consuming.

~~~~~~~~~~~~~

After each lesson, I was so happy that I wanted to share my experiences with everyone I knew. I'd call Kay, who lived across the street from me and had a daughter the same age as mine. "Would you like to come over for a glass of wine this afternoon?"

She'd agree, and our children would play together while I would enthuse. But Kay, like most of my friends, really wasn't interested in my incessant chatter about the joy of flight.

I really wanted to find female flying buddies. I had heard that there was a local club of women pilots. I could hardly wait until I became a certificated private pilot so I could get acquainted with them. But there were a few hurdles to pass first.

Each certificate, and some ratings, requires passing a written test. Nowadays, that isn't such a difficult task, because the FAA publishes all the possible test questions. There are lots of questions to study, but if you work diligently, it is easy to get a good score.

Back in the years when I was earning my ratings, however, the FAA tried to keep all the tests a big secret. There was a company that would pay people to remember the test questions and pass them on for publication. This wasn't considered quite fair.

Fortunately, the FAA finally recognized that if a person knew the answers to all the possible questions, that meant he or she had learned quite a bit about flying. Companies began offering printed guides containing the questions and the answers, and everyone bought a copy of these publications for each written test they took.

During "my time," before these guides became available, a passing grade (at least 70%) was not a sure thing. Of course, I had read the textbook and attended private pilot ground school. I passed a few quizzes in the process. Yet, when I mentioned the test, people shook their heads. The test was widely dreaded.

At the time, the local Flight Service Station administered the exams. I walked in, recommendation from my instructor in hand, and introduced myself to the person in charge of written tests that day. He brought out the application and began filling it in for me. He asked how many times I had taken it before, and I announced that it was my first. Fortunately, I didn't make any comment about planning to pass it, because he then said he'd already flunked it twice.

Well, I didn't get a perfect score, but I passed it easily. Another obstacle cleared.

The last hurdle was passing the "practical" exam, which means an oral and a flight test. Since I didn't have any pals at the airport yet, I didn't know anyone to ask about this dreaded ordeal. I kind of thought that getting information from someone who had experienced it would be cheating a bit anyway.

I wasn't afraid of tests; I had a college education and have usually done well on exams. It's just that, other than a very few rides as a passenger, aviation had been totally outside my experience until a few months before.

Maurine was the FAA-designated examiner used by Apollo, the flight school I was attending. A designated examiner is an accomplished pilot and experienced flight instructor selected by the FAA to conduct practical exams for various certificates and ratings. Unlike the FAA examiners, they aren't employed by the federal government, so they charge for their services. But using a designated examiner allowed me to take the test at my local airport, saving the expense and nerve-wracking experience of flying to the closest district office (Van Nuys, an extremely busy airport).

I'd had a couple of glimpses of Maurine prior to my test, but I didn't know her. She had a regular job at the University of California, Santa Barbara, and visited the flight school only on days when someone was scheduled for a checkride. If passed, the oral and flight tests result in a certificate or rating that allows a person to fly with new privileges. In my case, I would be a real, certified private pilot!

Maurine was known to be tough but fair. That sounded all right to me. The routine was to meet her at the flight school, where she would check all the paperwork required of an applicant. She then would assign a trip for me to plan, allowing thirty minutes for completion. We got along; she was happy with my required paperwork, and she assigned a flight. We chatted a little more. I was enjoying our chat immensely, until she suddenly announced that I had used up 10 of my 30 minutes.

I overcame my astonishment at what I saw as a dirty trick and raced through my preparations, finishing just in time. She checked my calculations and pronounced them adequate; then we went out to the airplane. I had preflighted it earlier, but of course she wanted to check my procedure, so I did it again.

The flight went well, although she gave me no feedback during our time in the air. The first segment was starting the cross-country that I had planned. This segment lasted until I had climbed to my chosen altitude and she was convinced that I knew how to get there and had properly done some calculations about how the wind was affecting the airspeed. Then I had to calculate a revised time of arrival at the destination.

Since we were now at a few thousand feet above the ground, I was asked to perform all the usual maneuvers: flight at minimum controllable airspeed, steep turns, various kinds of stalls, and others, with an emphasis on "hood work": flying without seeing outside.

A hood obstructs vision except for the airplane's instruments, located on what would be called a dashboard in a car. I had had the standard three hours of instruction in being able to fly out of a cloud should I suddenly encounter one. Obviously, flying through clouds was a situation to be avoided as a non-instrument rated pilot. Not only would it be unsafe, it was illegal without an instrument rating. But it was still important to practice in case such a situation ever came up.

As we returned to the airport, Maurine gave me the choice of performing either a short field or a soft field landing. No, we didn't actually go to a short or soft (because of snow or grass) landing strip. These conditions would be simulated, of course. There are no dinky runways or non-hard surfaced runways at Santa Barbara Airport.

The Piper Cherokee 140 lends itself to nice short field approaches but is not so amenable to soft techniques. At the time, I thought I was just not as good at the soft maneuver—I didn't know that this is true for most everyone. So I hesitated a little and then chose a short field. Maurine undoubtedly chuckled to herself at my pretended indecision.

I landed just past the spot Maurine assigned and brought the airplane to a stop quite efficiently. Maurine reached over and congratulated me! I asked, "Do you mean that I passed?"

She was surprised that I couldn't tell, but how could I? Although the standards for short field landings and all the other maneuvers were published in a little pamphlet called the Flight Test Guide—so many miles per hour, so many feet, etc.—I wasn't sure how well I'd performed in her eyes. Later, when I was testing private pilots myself, I knew that it really wasn't a subjective assessment. But I didn't know that yet.

Chapter 3

It's Fun Being a Pilot

The day after I became a certified private pilot, I went to the airport and signed up for an airplane. As I was preflighting, several people stopped by. After congratulating me, they asked what I was doing, since there was no passenger present. I said I was going to see if I could still fly.

Nobody found that funny, and they all thought it was odd. They told me that from now on, I should be taking other people flying, not soloing.

Well, I thought about that, but I continued my preparation and then took off. It was a lovely flight—no worrying about checkrides or critiques, just a peaceful, joyous trip into the beautiful sky. It felt great being up there, leaving other humans and buildings behind. They grew smaller and smaller until I forgot them for a while.

After I landed, the tranquil mood continued as I thought, *Oh yes, that was the joy of flying.* The exhilaration and peacefulness that I could enjoy without having to make conversation were priceless.

~~~~~~~~~~~~~~

Renting airplanes is expensive. There are some ways to cut costs, however. After I got my "license to learn," as people sometimes call the private pilot certificate, I checked out the options. Fixed base operators (FBOs), which offer many services at airports, have the most expensive rentals. They aren't philanthropic organizations; they exist to make money for the owners.

Another way to go is a flying club. I joined one that had four airplanes: a Cessna 150, a Cessna 172, and two Cessna 205s, one of which was the plane I first rode in when I learned to love the idea of flying. Clubs don't try to make a profit; their purpose is to make it a little cheaper for the members to take trips. I didn't learn until later that one of the ways this club economized was on maintenance, which was ultimately the reason I dropped out. No, nothing terrible happened to me, fortunately.

I checked out other airplanes, filling out a worksheet on the systems and procedures of a particular plane and flying a checkout flight with a flight instructor, who signed me off as a competent pilot in that type of plane—first in the Cessna 172, which was most similar to the plane in which I'd been as a student, then in a Piper Warrior. Both had 150-horsepower engines; the big difference was that while the Piper had low wings, the Cessna had high wings. This makes for handling differences, but it only took a couple of lessons to make the transition.

Later in my flying life, I could easily jump from one type of airplane to another, but at this point, it was harder. As a new pilot, flying an unfamiliar plane was a lot like trying to drive a car with a stick shift after learning on an automatic. Everything was in a slightly different place. The Cessna trim wheel wasn't where I was accustomed to reach for it. The instruments were pretty much the same, but the procedure for changing fuel tanks wasn't. Since the Cessna fuel tanks are located in wings above the fuselage, gravity fed the fuel to the engine, so no electric pump was needed. That meant I didn't need to think about using a second pump for routine operations. Checking the fuel tanks during the preflight involved climbing up on a little stool stashed in the back of the plane, rather than reaching across the low wings of Pipers.

Although it was challenging, it was fun flying a type of plane new to me, especially the Cessna 150. It was tiny and, while not powerful, it was quick to respond to the controls. Also, it could be spun legally. All planes can be spun, but some don't recover so well or simply haven't been tested past one turn and therefore aren't certified for spins. I loved spins and later came to enjoy flying on the slightly wild side: aerobatics.

Naturally, when I took passengers, I didn't engage in such antics. I began with very tame, short flights. My husband enjoyed our first little non-stop scenic trip to the harbor, although he never asked to go for another half-hour scenic jaunt. I think he really preferred longer trips to out-of-town destinations. Other people liked to get a good look at their town from above, and most loved getting a view of their home, which looked like a dollhouse from the sky.

My son Greg, who was seven, was eager to go, so I took him to the airport, got a Cessna 150 ready, and we took off. As soon as we were airborne, the door popped open! Being new to little Cessnas, I wasn't really expecting it and didn't prepare Greg for the possibility. My flight instructor had popped a door during my checkout to show how harmless it was and how easily it could be closed. But I didn't want to scare my child, so I aborted the takeoff when we were about 20 feet above the runway.

I'd always been told to abort the takeoff if anything at all goes awry, so I did. What I hadn't been told was how to do it. But I simply pulled off the power, adjusted the attitude and the trim, added full flaps, advised the tower, and landed farther down the runway.

We postponed our flight to another day. I didn't want him to be afraid and had a discussion with him about it on the way home. This didn't ruin flying for Greg; much later he became a commercial airline pilot.

My five-year-old daughter Christa was the easiest of passengers; she'd just go to sleep on flights of over 15 minutes. You might think this was a sign of trust in her mother's piloting ability, but actually, it was more about boredom.

We had relatives in San Francisco, so I flew my family up that way quite often. I say up that way because although SFO accommodated little airplanes, it wasn't until I was flying a high performance single that I felt I could keep up with the big planes on final approach to SFO. So, instead, we aimed for Half Moon Bay, which is close to San Francisco. But usually, because that airport is so often fogged in, we would divert to San Carlos. I learned two things on our first trip to San Carlos:

First, when Air Traffic Control (ATC) requests that a pilot should "Report the salt pile," it will be a reasonably apparent landmark, not the tiny mound that was my immediate mental picture when I first heard this phrase.

Second, even though a passenger is intelligent, observant, and helpful, this doesn't mean that he can be trusted. The controller informed me of my traffic and husband Bob said, "There it is." Well, no! There it wasn't! He was looking at another plane outside the traffic pattern.

I go back to that often quoted comment that a private pilot certificate is a license to learn. That is definitely what it is. I just hadn't realized how much more, aside from improving flying skills, needed to be learned.

~~~~~~~~~~~~

I took other people flying, too—quite a few. Not everyone was eager to go. Several of my friends who had assured me that they could hardly wait until I got my license turned out not to be so interested when the time came. That was fine; I didn't want to take reluctant passengers.

My good friend Marti agreed to go to Santa Maria with me. This was a good short flight, far away enough to be a real destination (50 miles as the crow flies) but not long enough to be boring. I really knew the ropes: where to park, what the combination was to get back onto the field after the flight, where to have lunch. You know, the things that suggested to passengers that I didn't need to be reading from the "how to fly" book.

Marti was game; she hid her nervousness well. The trip to Santa Maria was smooth and we had fun at lunch. I could tell she had been more anxious than I had initially observed, and also that her fears had been banished, because she fell asleep on the way home. This might not seem like a compliment, but it was.

What a lot of people don't realize is that a brand new private pilot is at a peak of competence, one which they many never achieve again unless they continue to hone their skills by working with an instructor toward another rating, or simply by flying, practicing the basics, and stretching their abilities.

One very neat flight involved a teenager I hardly knew. "Buckley" was the sixteen-year-old son of a friend of mine. I learned that he was best friends of the son of some people who had their own plane and that he had yearned for a ride.

I required his parents' permission, which they gave, and off we went. After takeoff and clearance to turn north toward Santa Ynez, I looked at Buckley and he said, "It's just like I dreamed it would be!" As I said, very neat.

~~~~~~~~~~~~~

I decided it was time to take a longer trip, and so I signed out the flying club's 172, N8841Z, for several days. I listed my destination as Pullman, Washington, where good friends lived.

This caught the attention of the club safety officer, a retired law enforcement officer who liked to bluster. He called me and demanded the particulars of my proposed flight. First of all, how many passengers? When I listed my husband and children, Harry launched into an interrogation. Apparently, I didn't realize that a Cessna 172 wasn't really a four-people craft. Had I worked a weight and balance problem? And was it true that I was a blonde? He didn't really voice that last thought, but it occurred to me that he might be thinking it.

I described my six- and eight-year-old children, including their modest weights. Then I read off the figures of the weight and balance calculation, which I had completed earlier. This defused Harry somewhat, but he requested the name of my flight instructor just to make sure I'd been adequately prepared. Well, okay, that's fair.

During my training, and afterward in my flying career, I encountered other incidents like this, where people would question my ability simply on the basis of my gender. I was sensitive to the unfairness and ignorance of this behavior and always reacted with determination to prove my ability and performance. Second best, merely because I was a woman, was never an acceptable supposition that I would entertain in any endeavor.

The summer that I became a private pilot was during the early 70s oil crisis. That came into play on our trip to Pullman, which is near Spokane and next to the Idaho border. That's quite a ways in a plane that flies 115 mph when level and slower when climbing or when approaching an airport.

It was easy enough to leave the home airport with full tanks. However, at that time, many companies where pilots stopped for fuel while enroute restricted the amount you could buy. A couple of places on my way to Pullman would only sell me 10 gallons a side. (Fuel is carried in tanks that are located in each wing. In the 172, the tanks could hold a total of 38 gallons.)

Twenty gallons isn't much when the plane averages about eight gallons an hour. This arbitrary rationing wasn't just annoying, it was counterproductive. It actually caused more gas to be consumed. Approaches and landings burn extra fuel, and takeoffs and climbs burn even more. And, of course, they also take time. I had to squander a lot of both on that trip.

Furthermore, we flew over some rather remote areas where the landmarks listed on the sectional might be mines or buildings, not the easiest to spot. I actually thought to myself that I hoped I knew what I was doing. Fortunately, but not surprisingly, I did.

As I approached Pullman, I called in for an airport advisory and requested that the FBO call the friends we were visiting and tell them we'd be ready to be picked up in 45 minutes. The frequency I used was Unicom, which is assigned to many FBOs all through the country.

At larger airports, regular personnel man Unicom. At little ones such as Pullman/Moscow (Idaho) Airport, I was answered by a friendly and helpful airport bum. (Airport bum is a friendly name for those of us who love to hang out at airports even when we don't have a particular reason for being there.) He obliged me with the advisory and call request, then asked if I'd like to see his new plane, a Decathlon—a nice aerobatic model. I said sure; then I realized I had to renege, saying that I had my family along. I suddenly realized that jaunts involving family would be of a more scheduled variety than my usual casual wanderings by myself or with other pilots.

We had a grand time with our friends. Kay and Phil had a daughter, Michelle, who was the same age as Greg, and a son, Chris, who was the same age to the day as our Christa. So the kids enjoyed the chance to play and the grownups chatted and laughed, free of the need to deal with bored or cranky kids.

Still, I did visit the airport every day. The first time, I drove out to move the plane to a different tiedown. Much to my dismay, the plane wouldn't start. It wouldn't even try. I walked to the local maintenance shop and explained my plight. A friendly mechanic promised to look at it later that day. He did and called me to say that the battery was simply in need of water. Phew! I hoped that was all that was wrong and just to be sure, went out the next day and flew around the pattern. I was relieved, but I did worry about the fact that the mechanic had spelled *water* with two t's.

Phil and his kids were eager to go for a hop in the 172. They had an appointment in nearby Lewiston and we decided we'd all go, some by car and others in the plane. I took Phil, Michelle, and Chris first, and it was a big success. A half hour was the perfect length of time for the kids.

Then came the return trip. I don't remember who all went with me on this one except for Kay. I could read on her face that she really didn't want to go, but felt that she should because if it wasn't safe enough for her, why had she allowed the little children to face the danger?

So she climbed aboard and we made the quick trip. As I always did when taking passengers for their first flights with me at the controls, I explained what I was doing when it seemed appropriate or interesting. I'd found that it was good to describe why I was reducing power, with its decrease in sound, in order to assure folks that the plane wasn't having a catastrophic engine failure. So I said something like, "Since we are approaching Pullman, I'm going to pull back the throttle as we descend..."

Kay retorted, "I don't care what you have to do. I just want to be on the ground."

Not everyone loves flying. Kay did, however, go on a couple of other flights with me later. She's a practical person, and if the flight served a purpose, she enjoyed it. For example, viewing whales cavorting in the Pacific Ocean and visiting Catalina Island were very acceptable reasons to fly.

~~~~~~~~~~~~~

"Airport Bums – Try to learn from the mistakes of others. You won't live long enough to make all of them yourself."

Since I had the luxury of being a stay-at-home mom when my children were little, I had a lot of spare time to spend at the airport while they were in school. This allowed me to become a full-fledged airport bum. In fact, I still have a t-shirt with a comical drawing and the words "International Order of Airport Bums." There were about a half dozen of us who sported those shirts. Just me and five guys.

We spent hundreds of hours soaking up the atmosphere and sharing stories.

The senior member was a nice retired man named Tom McKenna who had flown taildraggers for thousands of hours, had been a barnstormer, and loved to perform aerobatics. He knew all the old bold pilots of similar bents. He had a million great stories. Although he was in his seventies, Tom bought and flew several acrobatic Citabrias over five or ten years.

Another steady member was Tom Z, a disabled cop (injured back) who spent parts of several days a week hanging around and occasionally renting an airplane for a joy ride. He also loved aerobatics but wasn't anywhere nearly as proficient as Old Tom. He was funny, though, and he drew wicked cartoons of airport exploits, featuring easily recognizable local airport characters.

~~~~~~~~~~~~~~

Aviation is not so much a profession as it is a disease. The lure of the airport for me became a family joke. If we drove past an airport or even saw a sign pointing toward one, the kids urged me to keep going straight and cheered the times when I resisted the urge to turn toward it.

It was true; I loved airports. Familiar ones, new ones—they were all magnets. Of course, I spent hours of non-flying, non-working time at Santa Barbara Airport. But while I was learning to fly, I would often drive to Santa Ynez to hang around—watch the glider operations, talk to other visitors, and assess the quality of the amateur landings.

The Santa Paula Airport was really fun to visit on the weekends. It was only an hour's drive from my home and provided hours of entertainment. The runway was always busy on a clear, not-too-windy Saturday or Sunday. Windy days provided fewer operations, but they could be thrilling to the onlookers. The location of the narrow, short landing strip, nestled near the foothills, made for squirrelly conditions. There were quite a few light taildraggers based there, and the pilots who were not so nimble would display staggering approaches, sometimes abandoning the attempt halfway down the runway, going around to try again or leaving to find a less challenging piece of asphalt.

At a little, uncontrolled airport like Santa Paula, an addicted would-be pilot such as I could sit down quite close to the action on the runway and nobody minded. Once, I arose from the ramp after a fascinating hour or so of watching precarious landings to find that my pants were soaked through with tar. I became more selective of my "parking" places.

~~~~~~~~~~~~~~

Soon after I obtained my private pilot certificate, a friend told me about another woman who was planning to take her private checkride. We got together so that she could hear all about my recent test.

Marilyn Weixel and I would probably never have become friends except for aviation. It's unlikely that we would even have run into each other: she was working on her Master's degree at UCSB, and I was a mom. However, we both were completely hooked on flying and spent hour after hour discussing all sorts of aviation trivia. When she graduated, instead of putting her new degree to work, she got a job at the same FBO where I flew and hung out during many of the hours that my children were in school.

I learned that there were quite a few women pilots in the Santa Barbara area, and that many of them belonged to a club: the Ninety-Nines. I was invited to a once-a-month meeting and became a member. The 99s, not 99ers as in 49ers, is an international organization, founded in 1929 by 99 licensed women pilots. Amelia Earhart was the first president. Read more about the 99s in the online appendix: http://www.awomansplaceisinthecockpit.com/appendix

It was great to be with a bunch of other women who were into aviation. I could babble about the joy of flying without catching daggers from wives of men who kind of wanted to be pilots. The women who had been flying for years smiled and remembered how exciting it was when they first flew.

We came from all different backgrounds, flying being the one thing we had in common. There were housewives, teachers, nurses, engineers, a mechanic's apprentice, a few wealthy women, and some who needed to carefully save up their dollars before indulging in their next flights. Not all members were active pilots, but everyone held at least a private pilot certificate.

Our chapter met once a month, usually at somebody's home, often including a potluck. Every Wednesday, there was a table reserved for us at a local restaurant a mile from the airport. Sometimes there would be lots of us there and occasionally just two or three.

It wasn't as much fun if a man joined us. He might try to give us helpful advice, even though he was a private pilot while some of us had commercial certificates and many times the number of flight hours he had.

We were proud of our WASP members. WASP stands for Women Airforce Service Pilots. These gals weren't really in the military, but they delivered planes to airfields where the men would fly them, and they towed targets for men who were practicing with live ammunition. You know, safe flights.

Once the war was over, they were dismissed, and it wasn't until many years later that they received the recognition they deserved. There is a great deal of information about them on this website: http://www.wingsacrossamerica.us/.

~~~~~~~~~~~~~~

The Ninety-Nines sponsored lots of activities. Local chapters, including ours, provided the service of air marking airfields. This is done to identify airports by painting the name of an airport on a ramp or taxi way. There is an interesting history to this program: it was the first US government program conceived, planned, and directed by a woman with an all-woman staff. The program was a part of the Bureau of Air Commerce.

In 1933, Phoebe F. Omlie was appointed Special Assistant for Air Intelligence of the National Advisory Committee for Aeronautics. She convinced the chief of the Airport Marking and Mapping Section of the Bureau of Air Commerce to start a program where each state would participate and better identify its towns and cities from the air. Each state was divided into sections of 20 square miles. A marker with the name of the nearest town was painted on the roof of the most prominent building and, if possible, at each 15-mile interval. If the towns were far apart, white painted markers, such as rocks and bricks, were used on the ground between them.

At the time the program was established, pilots generally flew without radios, which would have enabled them to identify air routes. With the aid of markers, even the most inexperienced pilots could verify where they were, even without a radio.

The program was funded by the Works Progress Administration. This was the first appropriation of funds specifically set up to aid private pilots, and it was hoped that the program would provide jobs for the unemployed and would establish valuable permanent airway aids.

Phoebe chose five leading women pilots as field representatives for the program: Louise Thaden, Helen Richey, Blanche Noyes, Nancy Harkness, and Helen McCloskey, all of whom were very well known in aviation.

World War II put a stop to the program. After the bombing at Pearl Harbor in 1941, the US Government decided that marked airports along the east and west coast were obvious targets for enemy identification and attack. As a result, Blanche Noyes, who had set about the work of marking some 13,000 sites, went about the work of blacking out those very markings she and her team of women pilots had diligently created.

After the war, Blanche Noyes was in charge of the Air Marking division of the Civil Aeronautics Administration. She believed that it was critical to not only replace the airport markings that were removed during the war for security reasons, but also to add even more navigational aids. And thus, the work began all over again.

Some of the letters in the airport name can be 50 feet tall. The Ninety-Nines labeled airports based on need, which often took them far from their local areas. When Ninety-Nines members in Alaska did air markings one year, some members traveled up to 300 air miles to meet at the designated airport to perform their work.

Funding for air marking no longer comes from the federal government. After Blanche Noyes's husband was killed in the crash of his Beachcraft Staggerwing, Blanche began to devote her energies to the Air Marking Program as a way of overcoming her grief. She became one of its most ardent supporters, so much so that when the federal funds for the program ran out, she flew all over the country to gain financial support from local chambers of commerce and civic groups.

The Ninety-Nines have continued air marking through the years. Airports or local governments or businesses will usually supply the paint, and the women pilots supply the tools and do the work. The chapter I belonged to in Santa Barbara did this several times at other airports.

Belonging to the organization gave me the chance to meet many other women who were passionate about flying. Sometimes chapters, as the local groups are called, will get together with other chapters. One group will fly to another's airport for lunch or another activity. Twice a year, members of several states join to hold meetings that combine fun and conducting the inevitable business generated by organizations. Once a year, there is an international meeting, usually in the USA.

The Southwest Section, which is the group of states my chapter belonged to, always had a meeting called a sectional (the same name as the maps we used for VFR navigation) in the spring and in the fall. The spring of 1975, my friend Rachel and I flew to the several-day meeting, which was held in Phoenix.

Rachel and I alternated legs flying a Cessna 172 to Tucson to participate in the 1975 Tucson Treasure Hunt, which occurred prior to the event in Phoenix. She flew from Santa Barbara to Blythe, and I took over from Blythe to Tucson, where we spent the night with a bunch of other Treasure Hunters.

Early the next morning, I flew and Rachel navigated, using the clues we'd been given. She had done this before and loved doing it.

We searched for each target, wrote down the answer—sometimes airports, sometimes altitudes relative to position, other times the result of solving a navigation problem, and many other things—then went on to the next. The route took us to Phoenix Sky Harbor, where there were so many little planes landing that we were assigned the right side of the runway and another was given the left. I was glad to have the right because most pilots tend to land left of their aiming point. I made sure not to impinge on the other plane's territory. When I asked the tower controller if it was customary to divide the runway this way, he said, "No, just for you."

We joined hundreds of other women for the Ninety-Nines convention, staying two nights. There were lots of activities planned and we especially enjoyed the ones based on aviation. Rather than watch a fashion show, for instance, Joan and Marilyn and I made appointments for glider lessons at the little Turf airport.

I flew us there in the 172. The runway was so rough that it was hard to find a good place to set down. But we did, and then carefully steered our way to the ramp.

We parked the plane and walked toward a group of men. One of them asked where our pilot was. I raised my hand and he grudgingly allowed, "Nice landing."

Little non-commercial airports are a great playground for old guys who like to pretend that women can't fly very well.

~~~~~~~~~~~~~~

The Ninety-Nines sponsor air races. Some are for both men and women, but a few are flown only by women, either solo or in two-person teams. The most famous of these was the annual Powder Puff Derby, a women's race that was flown many years from 1929 through 1977. It was a handicapped transcontinental race. Learn more about these races in the online appendix: http://www.awomansplaceisinthe-cockpit.com/appendix

I flew my Bonanza with Joan Steinberger as copilot in the 1976 race. Joanie would have dearly loved to win; she was a veteran of several Powder Puffs. I just wanted to have fun. To have a chance to win, the race route needed to be pre-flown in order to avoid the pitfalls of missing landmarks. Flying the race itself was expensive, and flying the course twice or more was prohibitive unless a team had a wealthy and generous sponsor. We didn't.

It was also exhausting. The rules required that all flying had to be done under VFR (Visual Flight Rules) conditions. We would get up for a 4:00 a.m. weather briefing, only to find that part of the route was

IFR because of clouds, fog, or low visibility. We would have checked out of our hotel and couldn't go back there to sleep. So we'd sit around the airport, checking the weather often, until we were pretty certain that we wouldn't encounter any disqualifying clouds or low visibilities. Sometimes, that didn't happen until the next day. We got very tired but were buoyed up by the excitement, and when we took off we felt refreshed and eager.

Our flight was from Sacramento, California, to Wilmington, Delaware, but not in a straight line. The course was determined by which airports would sponsor a stop.

Most of the stops were mandatory, although a few could be flown over before continuing to the next. Each city that offered a stop also provided motel reservations. These were a bit tricky to plan—if we were impeded by weather, we wouldn't get as far as we'd anticipated in a day.

We were required to finish the race in a stated number of days. Timing was accomplished by a record of takeoff times and clocking when we flew by specific points before arriving at certain airports.

In earlier years, the time was counted between takeoffs and landings, but the clock wasn't stopped until the pilots ran over and checked in after landing. This practice fostered the sudden cooling of engines, which does not promote long engine life. It was discontinued in favor of the flyby system.

With the flyby system, each airplane was assigned a number. The number, taped to the plane itself, was about the size of the plane's N number, so that spotters could read it. As we crossed the flyby point, the spotters would record our time. Then we could baby the airplane before and after landing by reducing power gradually and taxiing slowly to the tiedown area before shutting down the engine, which had worked hard that day.

People assumed that the airplanes suffered from being raced. That isn't true. As long as they were not overcooled by poorly planned descents, they actually benefitted from the races. Airplane engines like to be flown hard.

For regular flights, planes are usually operated at about 75% to 85% power for fuel economy and optimum range. This would be about 15 gallons an hour in my Bonanza. Flying flat out, full power, would result in 22 or 23 gallons per hour. It's quite an expensive difference.

As long as the engine was leaned properly, it loved the workout. The engine that propelled the Bonanza on the Derby, as well as during some other hard flying, achieved nearly 1800 hours (rather than the expected 1500) before needing an overhaul. Pilots often fly their engines gently, thinking that will be good for them. They are surprised to hear that brisk exercise benefits airplanes, just as people benefit from exercising.

People wondered what made women want to race. We were interviewed by various entities. One interviewer told me that, while many female pilots babbled about the beauty of flight and achieving the difficult, when asked why they raced, the favorite answer she heard was, "To get out of the house!"

I recognized some truth in this. It had only been a couple of years earlier that I had first taken a weekend off from raising kids and keeping house, and checked into a motel in a nearby city by myself. Some of my friends were shocked that I would do this, although our husbands enjoyed fishing trips of several days without wives.

Along the race, I was amazed to discover that we were cheered by groupies at each stop. The groupies were all men—not male pilots, but men who were fascinated by us.

By the time we had achieved the ability to fly airplanes, we had taken this skill for granted. It was an odd experience to be placed on a pedestal for having that ability.

~~~~~~~~~~~~~~~

I often hung out in the airport in the mornings, while my children were in school. One morning in October 1975, the owner of a lease-back Cessna 150 entered the FBO office to check out his plane and make a short flight. He hadn't flown for a while, so the dispatcher asked him to update his paperwork.

There was some problem; perhaps his medical wasn't current. Therefore, he couldn't be pilot-in-command. He noticed me hanging around and asked if I had an hour. Sure—I had two or three. I agreed to be the PIC for his short flight.

The mission was to find a little radio-controlled airplane that disappeared from sight the day before, not far from the airport. He thought it had landed in a tree and hoped to spot it from above. He said we'd go as soon as he informed the FBO office that I would be the official pilot for the flight.

This guy was rather casual, and I didn't think he had preflighted the airplane, but I didn't want to challenge him on it. I knew the plane flew every day and had been recently checked, but I definitely did want to at least make sure there was adequate fuel and oil.

I knew I didn't have much time, so I quickly checked the oil level and then headed for one of the fuel tanks. Usually, you use a step stool to access the fuel cap on top of the high-wing planes, but I didn't want to take the time, so I jumped up on the wing strut, right where it intersects the fuselage. I opened the cap, saw that the tank was full, replaced the cap… and fell off! I hurt a little bit, but I didn't think much about it, and soon we were in the air.

It was fun; we got permission from the tower to fly low over the orange groves where the little aircraft might be. The area was within the landing patterns for two of the runways, so we had to depart briefly for a couple of arrivals. But when we could return, we circled until we spotted the remote-control plane nestled in the upper branches of an orange tree in a nearby orchard. We took note of its exact position.

We landed, he thanked me, and that was the adventure.

Then I realized I was really hurting. It turned out I had fractured my tailbone. There is really not much that can be done about that. You can't put it in a cast, and I didn't want to take pain meds that might keep me on the ground. I was sore for weeks, but somehow, luckily, it never bothered me when I was flying.

This was much like the time I cracked my ribs. Our family drove northwest of town to a park that sported pretty little waterfalls after a good rain. I was playing in a very climbable tree with my young daughter while my son and husband went on a short hike. I told Christa not to go up to the branch she was eyeing because it didn't look too sturdy. Then, thinking only of my daughter's safety, I moved to that branch so that she could pass me and go a little higher. Of course, the branch broke and I fell out of the tree.

Ribs, like tailbones, are hard to set. Again, I was uncomfortable for weeks and again, being in an airplane magically caused the pain to recede—at least in my head. I always felt better, mentally and physically, when I was in an airplane.

Chapter 4

Spreading My Wings

Three of my pilot girlfriends and I went to Northrup Institute of Technology in Los Angeles, a maintenance training school, for a weekend workshop focusing on the 29 maintenance items that owners could legally perform on their own airplane. None of us planned to actually perform these things on a routine basis; none of us even had planes of our own then. We just wanted to learn more! More! MORE!

It was great fun. A display of worn and dirty spark plugs gave us a lot of information about what happens to them and when they must be replaced rather than just cleaned. We learned how to pack wheel bearings; and we did pack bearings and a lot of other things that I don't recall.

Most exciting, however, was our visit to LAX Air Traffic Control Tower. We had learned that we very probably wouldn't be admitted, and the guard we encountered confirmed this. Out of the blue, I asked him to call with our request to visit and let the controllers know that we were four young women. The other girls were all in their 20s and attractive. My friends thought it wouldn't help, but it did.

We went up to the tower cab and got a lot of attention. They answered all of our questions. One answer disappointed us: none of them were pilots. But the view from any tower cab is very interesting and LAX, with its huge amount of traffic, was spellbinding to us.

It was getting dark, and we answered their queries of what we planned to do for nightlife. These were nice guys, but our lack of interest in flirting was not what they had hoped. We were dedicated airport bums! We wanted to learn as much as we could about how this vast airport worked. We all expressed our desire to visit Los Angeles Approach Control. Despite some rolling of eyes over our priorities, they arranged for that, too. We had another great hour or so.

Just like any other job that is performed by experienced experts, it was a joy to witness. We got to walk from radar screen to radar screen and learned a lot. Radar controllers pass airplanes along from sector to sector, screen to screen. They send notes to each other advising of the handoffs. It was fun watching the progress of the various planes. It is really too bad that one of the aftereffects of 9/11 was disallowing visits to FAA Air Traffic Control facilities. It was a very educational experience that I always arranged for students before 2001.

Since we were staying very close to the airport, we spent a great portion of the night running to the window to watch all the 747s (relatively new to the skies then) that landed. Most people avoid airport noise; we reveled in it.

One small irony of this trip is that we didn't fly to get there. Sometimes a car is a more efficient mode of transportation, even when going to an aviation event. That was the case for this workshop.

Because my car was a big Buick station wagon, a typical mom's car in the 70s, I drove. Before the other girls arrived at my home at 6:00 a.m., I quickly removed kid stuff from the car and backed out of the garage. I didn't want to awaken the rest of the household with four excited heads spewing giggles.

The problem was that I didn't close the right side door on the Buick before backing out. I ended up causing quite a bit of damage to the little Datsun parked next to it, which my husband drove to work. When I surveyed my mess, the Buick was barely scratched, and I determined that the Datsun seemed fine for driving. Even the door I had plowed into still operated OK, so I just drove off.

That night, after the workshop, I called my husband to share the wondrous events of the day. He listened patiently until I finished and then asked, "What happened to my car?"

My enthusiasm for the activities of the day had completely wiped my two-car/single-driver collision out of my mind. Of course, I apologized for my thoughtlessness and turned down Bob's offer to call the insurance company. I could at least make the embarrassing report myself.

We used State Farm, which advertised that if their customers were involved in an accident with another vehicle insured by State Farm, the deductible portion would be waived. So when I called, I asked, "What if both of the cars were ours?"

I was surprised to hear that the waiver still applied. We didn't have to pay anything for the repairs!

~~~~~~~~~~~~~~

During the first years after earning my private pilot certificate (1973 and 1974), I flew a variety of airplane types. Cessnas and Pipers were fun, but I really wanted to fly a Bonanza. Known as doctor killers, they are powerful and fast Beechcraft single-engine dream planes. My physician husband would ride in one, but he didn't fly it. He decided not to learn to fly.

Despite their reputation, the planes aren't the killers. It's the godlike attitude of some of the doctor pilots who fly them.

I was extremely fortunate to be able to become a partner in a blue and white V35B, a v-tailed Bonanza. I had a demonstration flight in a brand new Bonanza and was dazzled. While the plane is challenging in some situations, it is fun to fly and a delight to land, even the first time.

The demo plane was equipped with a throw-over yoke, meaning that only one of the pilot seats had access to the aileron and elevator controls, although both had rudder pedals. Well, here I was, a private pilot that the salesman, Cliff, didn't know. He let me take off and play around, but he thought I should throw the controls back to him for landing.

I bargained with him: if the approach wasn't to his liking, I would go around and give it back to him. Cliff was a very experienced military pilot and flight instructor, and he agreed. The plane allowed me a graceful touchdown. I was hooked.

A low-key, nice-guy salesman, Bob Holmes found several possibilities of used Bonanzas for purchase. He and I flew a rental Comanche to San Jose, where we saw a few. I fell in love with N886T. The salesman in San Jose had flown it for a number of hours and even won a national precision flying contest with it. It was well tweaked. He flew it to Santa Barbara, where a local maintenance facility checked it out. My potential partner concurred with my choice, and it was ours!

Did I say that it was easy to fly? It was, but it could also be quite slippery, being designed for speed.

Some years later, there was a big to-do about V-tail Bonanzas like mine experiencing their tails failing and the planes crashing. It was true. People overstressed the tails, and they failed at very high speeds when the pilots lost control of the aircraft. I have included more about the V Tailed Bonanza in the online appendix: http://www.awomansplaceisinthecockpit.com/appendix

A high-performance plane requires a high-performance pilot. The FAA enacted a new regulation requiring a high-performance checkout for people flying such aircraft. The problem was, there were several different reasons why a plane could have that high-performance designation. It could have more than 200 horsepower, or it could have a constant speed propeller, flaps, and retractable landing gear.

In order to make a low-performance Piper Cub meet the requirements to be a high-performance plane, you could modify the plane in two different ways. You could either give it a 201-horsepower engine and keep everything else the same, or you could let it keep its 40-horsepower engine and add a controllable pitch prop, flaps, and retractable gear.

Training in one of these options certainly wouldn't prepare a pilot to fly the other, yet it would be allowed. That's why the FAA eventually separated the two options into complex and high- performance checkouts—a very wise move. A high-performance airplane is one that has more than 200 horsepower. A complex airplane is one that has retractable landing gear, controllable pitch propeller, and adjustable flaps.

I have included more about the V-Tailed Bonanza in the appendix. One strange thing is that investigations of many V-Tail accidents revealed that the landing gear was never extended. I've often wondered, why not? Was it because there was a maximum gear extension speed, and these events would always have exceeded that speed?

That would be so sad, because extending the gear acts as a big speed brake. It also stabilizes the airplane. The possible damage that would occur from exceeding the speed would have been just to the gear doors; Beech landing gear is famously strong. And people wouldn't have died.

I always included this information when I checked out pilots in a Bonanza. Once I became a flight instructor, I was known as a Bonanza expert, so I did a lot of those.

~~~~~~~~~~~~~

Weather forecasts are horoscopes with numbers.

Santa Barbara, where I learned to fly, is located in southern California along the Pacific coastline. While this provides a great climate that produces temperatures in the 70s most days, it also subjects the area to bouts of fog very often. This is most pronounced over the ocean and slightly inland—just where the airport is located.

Because fog is so common, it's a big factor in deciding whether to fly or not. Weather for local flight is pretty predictable, and being close to the airport allows a quick return if the weather starts to deteriorate. But, of course, most people don't learn to fly just to tour the local skies. It's all about trips to other places.

Fog is quirky. While Flight Service does a good guess based on sound meteorology, forecasts aren't always accurate. It is common to return to SBA after hours or days and find that the airport is covered with a white layer, obscuring the airport and making VFR flight illegal.

Fortunately, right across the mountains that border Santa Barbara to the north is Santa Ynez Airport, which is usually clear and makes a fine alternate.

However, it was inconvenient to land in Santa Ynez and have to figure out how to get home. There were rental cars available, and *that* was convenient. What was inconvenient was that both the rental car and the airplane needed to be returned to their homes soon. This required either time or money. Someone else could drive or fly them back, but they often needed to be paid to do so.

The answer to this dilemma is the Instrument Rating, which allows a pilot to fly through clouds and fog, as long as the destination airport is forecast to be above the minimums of ceiling and visibility required by the approach procedure. The addition of this rating to a pilot certificate provides a great deal of flexibility. While the weather still needs to be considered carefully, the extra qualification allows a pilot to decide to make many more trips. Often, it isn't even needed, but it is a great piece of paper to have in your wallet should an instrument approach be required.

It is also quite a project. While the private pilot license is all about learning to fly while getting a lot of feedback through the senses, flying in the clouds is very different. It is very disorienting when you can't automatically verify that the airplane is flying straight and level, climbing or descending as planned, or executing the banked turn that you desire. Instead, a pilot has to rely on the gauges: instruments similar to what you might see on the dashboard of your car, with a few crucial additions.

The good thing is that a well-trained instrument pilot who maintains the strict level of currency required to fly in the clouds can perform very well and confidently. (Currency is recent hours of flying by reference to the instruments, without access to the view outside the aircraft.) In fact, one time when driving my teenage children and myself to a vacation destination, I encountered actual smoke from a fire. I automatically "went to the gauges." That wasn't a solution to the problem, but as I drove out of the brief area of blindness, I had to laugh at my reaction.

The process of obtaining the IFR rating is just as big a commitment as earning the private pilot certificate. In fact, most people find it more difficult.

It certainly is different. There are new procedures and new regulations, and you have to learn to trust the instruments, rather than your body. When deprived of sight outside the aircraft, a common reaction is to think you are in a 30 degree bank when you are actually level (or vice versa). Once I started instructing instrument students, I always made sure that each of them experienced this, preferably in the actual clouds. Until that happened, they didn't really believe it could happen to them.

I spent a few months earning my instrument rating and I found it fascinating. There was so much to learn and I always wanted to know everything. I would try to schedule an instrument lesson at the last minute on days when there was a thick layer of fog over the area. Since instructors sometimes cancelled landing practice sessions for primary students on those days, I often could take advantage of a schedule opening.

IFR clearances are more complex than the takeoff and landing clearances that begin and end VFR flights. They are logical, but it takes a while to decipher them. It takes longer yet to get up to speed on copying them. The controller who gives your clearance may talk fast or slow. You have to read the clearance back to demonstrate that you've understood. Since you will be using your clearance for navigation, it is crucial that you get it right.

In days past, it was not required to read back the clearance, but after people (including Frank Sinatra's mother) died as a result of a pilot making an incorrect assumption and just saying "OK," it became mandatory to do so.

Fortunately, pilot supplies shops offer a recording of clearances, to help pilots get familiar with them. The recording starts with simple instructions spoken slowly. Gradually, it moves to complicated ones uttered quite rapidly. I spent hours practicing until I became adept. And then, once I was receiving actual IFR cross-country clearances, I discovered that they were easier because I had planned the trip and was familiar with the airways and points in the clearances.

While I worked on earning my IFR ticket, I flew with several instructors. Certified flight instructors often move on to the charter department, making them unavailable to students.

Flying with more than one instructor gave me the benefit of several points of view. I even based the plane at Oxnard Airport for a week or so in order to fly with a designated examiner known for being picky but very knowledgeable. We did a bunch of flights to the LA area, where we could do a variety of instrument approaches to busy airports that were close to each other. That was a great experience.

On the other hand, perhaps because of flying with several instructors, nobody really controlled my course. And so I failed my checkride! Oh no! I blew a holding pattern. I caught it, but it was too late. Maurine asked if I wanted to continue the test. I said yes because I felt that I had nothing to lose; I'd already flunked at the very beginning.

We did the rest of the requirements and all went well... except for going back to the airport, where people assumed I'd passed. Maurine asked if I wanted her to tell people and send them away. I was tempted, but I said no. They were all my friends.

It was very embarrassing. But, a few days later, I had the precious piece of paper that pronounced me an instrument pilot. Maurine told me that she was impressed that I put the error behind me on that first flight and flew well afterwards.

~~~~~~~~~~~~~~

I was very lucky to be able to spend a few years as a full-time mom. Because the children were now in school five days a week, I had plenty of time to play airport.

At that time in the 70s, a fixed base operation (FBO) had several departments: fueling and tiedowns, hangar rental, maintenance, charter, and flight school. Because I was at the airport a lot, I knew most everyone that worked at Apollo. They knew I had free time, so I was sometimes able to enjoy flights at little expense.

I occasionally occupied the back seat during a training flight of the charter pilots. This was an eye-opener. These guys whose skills were so far advanced from mine still needed to upgrade, and the training involved the same old things: heading and altitude. Of course, they were struggling to do this while identifying and troubleshooting failed engines in multiengine airplanes.

Apollo started a commuter airline, and this affected me in two ways. First, since I knew the charter pilots who advanced to airline pilots, there were more opportunities to ride along. While the guys were training for their Airline Transport Pilot certificate, the back seat of the twin-engine plane was sometimes available to me. Many people might not see the appeal of getting to observe training that involves a sweating pilot fighting to control a plane with a simulated engine loss while in the simulated clouds, but I loved it.

Once the airline was functional, I was able to get into a free seat to and from San Jose, the first destination for the infant airline, just for fun. On one occasion, I was invited to pick up the two pilots who ferried a Handley Page Jetstream (the kind of plane used for the airline) to Salinas for painting. The company paid for the direct expenses of my Bonanza for two trips and I got to fly by myself one way each trip. One of the professional pilots flew the other two legs, enjoying the swift little airplane's quick response.

I had recently earned my instrument rating, which came in very handy the day we flew back to the paint shop to pick up the newly painted Jetstream. We had checked the weather, of course, and the forecast for the flight back to Santa Barbara called for VFR until close to SBA, which would have a ceiling of 1000 feet, perfect for my first actual IFR solo.

I was excited about this new experience and feeling confident, having mentally rehearsed the steps I would use for each segment. The trip went well, and I was eager for the opportunity to enter the clouds and shoot the Instrument Landing System (ILS) approach into SBA. Shortly before requesting the IFR clearance, I requested a weather update and discovered that the Santa Barbara fog bank was lowering, approaching minimums.

Of course, I had options. I could land at severe clear, as pilots label days with unlimited visibility, in Santa Ynez and wait for better weather. Or, if I continued, I could begin the approach and miss it at any stage. If I didn't break out of the clouds at 210 feet, I would definitely declare a missed approach and go back to Santa Ynez.

Naturally, my new skills sharp, I took the IFR clearance, giving me an altitude and fix. I was to report Halibut intersection. This was followed by the question, "Beth, are you IFR legal now?"

I proudly confirmed my new status and added that I was alone in the plane.

"Bonanza 86T, cleared for the Santa Barbara ILS 7 approach. Report the outer marker."

Now I was on the localizer, descending to 1900 feet, where I stayed until the glide slope centered. I entered the clouds, without a hood! Simulating clouds under a hood is like pretending. I had flown through a fog layer several times before without the hood, but never while flying alone.

Fog doesn't seem static when flying through it. It comes at you and distracts you into wanting to check outside, even before the possibility of breaking out approaches. I stayed glued to the gauges, however, and my small corrections kept me right on target.

Somewhere between 250 and 220 ft., I encountered clear air and shifted my gaze to outside and, oh no! There was no runway in front of me! It took less than a second to remember that I had been flying a heading of about 090° to maintain the course of 073° as I neared the airport in order to correct for a crosswind.

So I shifted my gaze to the left, and there was Runway 7. Soon, I was on the ground, happy and proud.

~~~~~~~~~~~~~

I only knew one female flight instructor while I was learning to fly. Her name was Sheffie. She loved flying the mail in the middle of the night, alone with the Twin Beech, her little dog, and the sky.

Because she managed to do little training, I only had one informal ground session with her. My regular instructor and I were just returning to the office after a flight and he was debriefing me. He mentioned the wording of one of my communications with Santa Barbara Tower and advised me to use the proper phrasing. I remarked that what I had said was perfectly clear—so what if it wasn't proper?

After exchanging glances with my male instructor, Sheffie asked me to sit down and then said, "Look, you have two strikes against you being a woman. In order to get respect, you need to do everything better than expected, and that definitely applies to using the right words in the right order."

I never forgot that, and I passed that advice on to many students in later years.

I was making one of my trips from Santa Barbara to the Midwest when the weather deteriorated, so I asked for an instrument clearance. The male controller asked me to verify that I was qualified to fly IFR, and I affirmed my rating. He obliged and slowly read me my directions, "Bonanza 886 Tango is cleared to..." It was long and detailed, and I read it back to him fast and correctly.

Sheffie was right. I heard the change of attitude in the controller's voice as he said, "Clearance correct. Contact Denver Center. Good day."

On another flight to the Midwest, I ran into a similar situation. It was an IFR day. I needed to make an instrument approach into my destination. My localizer failed me, so I asked for the NDB approach.

Nobody chose an NDB approach unless there was no other option. The NDB uses an old-fashioned gadget called an ADF. The ADF needle points to the station, but it is wobbly and not at all precise. Both VOR and NDB approaches are called non-precision approaches, but compared to using the ADF, VOR approaches are quite reliable. The closer to the station, the more accurate they are.

On this flight, I could have requested a VOR approach, but it would have involved a lot more time because I was on the other side of the airport and would have had to be vectored a long way before intercepting the final approach course. I was on the right side for the NDB.

ATC cleared me for the NDB, which provoked a few airliners to ask ATC, "Where is that Bonanza?" assuming that I wouldn't be accurately following the course.

If I had been in another plane, I probably would have requested the lengthy VOR approach, but my Bonanza had an unusually accurate ADF, and I felt confident. Furthermore, Santa Barbara boasted an NDB approach that I used all the time, training IFR students.

One time, there was a power failure, which caused the failure of the ILS. I think it was United that was coming in to SBA, and the pilot had to use the NDB for the IFR approach. He missed it twice. Likely he hadn't spent much time practicing the NDB into SBA— probably none. He ended up going off course and to the north. That's where the mountains are, and that's where you get off course if you have a good ADF and you're a good pilot. Why would that be? Well, ADFs are full of errors which you can read about in the online appendix: http://www.awomansplaceisinthecockpit.com/appendix

Chapter 5

Ups and Downs

Not everyone thinks flying is neat.

During the time when I was earning my pilot certificates and ratings, before I became a flight instructor, my life outside of the airport consisted of being a wife and mother of two youngsters, friends with people who had children of similar ages to mine, friends with a bunch of couples with whom we shared interests, and friends with people from the church we attended. Some of these people envied my luck in being able to learn to fly. Some found it interesting; others were disapproving.

"Angie" fit into the last category. As the mother of three children, the younger two of whom were a boy and girl the ages of my children, she never missed an opportunity to tell me how irresponsible I was being by flying. "Do you at least have life insurance?" was an example of a not-so-subtle hint that I would likely be leaving my children motherless.

So I was very surprised to see Angie and her children at "A Day in the Sky," which sold people rides in airplanes to benefit a charity.

The FAA regulations allowed a private pilot with at least 200 hours of flight experience to be granted a waiver so that they could participate in flying these folks around. Those 200 hours could have been acquired over many years, which wouldn't make for a very adept pilot, or during a year or two, as in my case.

What really floored me was that when Angie saw me, she begged me to arrange to be the pilot for her children's excursion. I declined. Graciously, I hope, but I don't remember what I said.

~~~~~~~~~~~~~~

I had planned to learn some sign language, at least the alphabet, on our trip to Modesto. We were going to visit some good friends who were providing a home for a little girl who was profoundly deaf.

The trip would take about two hours, and in good weather, my husband could "drive" the airplane. That means that I could tell him a visual point to steer toward, and if I had it trimmed, the altitude would pretty much take care of itself. Of course, I'd be right there; I'd just be looking down at my notes a lot.

It was an easy plane to fly: a Cherokee 235, which I had rented because my Bonanza was in Oregon getting an engine overhaul. It was such a good engine that I elected to have it overhauled rather than get an exchange, which would have been faster.

This was a great plan if the sky were clear. That day, it definitely wasn't. There was about a thousand-foot ceiling, which would require flying IFR to get through to the blue sky above.

I always filed a complete flight plan to a destination where I knew the weather was sufficiently good to make an IFR approach, or to one with unrestricted cloudless skies. This habit ensured that if the communication radios should fail en route, I would have a cleared path to my destination. Fortunately, that was my habit, and I filed all the way to Modesto.

Obstacles began occurring as soon as I began the journey. The Piper Cherokee 235 that I had reserved, N40801, checked out fine during my preflight, taxi, and run-up. The only snarl before takeoff was that when the tower gave me my clearance, one of the en route points was a combination of numbers and letters that made sense neither to me nor to the controller who read it to me. I asked him what it was and he said he didn't know, but he could find out and amend the clearance once I was in the air.

I declined. Had I accepted the clearance as it was and then lost communications after flying through the cloud layer, I would have no complete route to follow. And Santa Ynez, just across the mountains from Santa Barbara, was having one of its fairly rare IFR days. There were no cloudless airports along my path for the day.

In a few minutes, ATC supplied me with a new clearance, one that had all the points covered. I was cleared for takeoff.

As I began climbing, Cherokee N40801's compass began spinning—not a good thing in instrument conditions. Of course, I had set the directional gyro (DG) to the compass before takeoff, but DGs can precess quite a bit. Because they are powered by spinning gyroscopes, they are subject to drift errors, so they need to be recalibrated to the magnetic compass frequently. (One might wonder why pilots don't just use the compass instead of the DG. Unfortunately, the magnetic compass has a bunch of errors on its own and gives correct readings only during straight and level flight.)

Fortunately, I had not entered the clouds yet, so I called the tower and requested a return. I was cleared to land on the runway from which I had just departed and touched down shortly thereafter.

After taxiing back to the FBO and tying the airplane down, I walked inside and asked if the other plane of the same model was available. It was. I quickly called the tower on the phone and explained that I would like to have them hold my flight plan and that everything would be the same except that instead of N40801, I would be flying Cherokee N32645 (sometimes abbreviated to 645).

I preflighted 645; my family moved our things to the replacement airplane. I followed the same procedure of clearance to taxi, run-up, IFR clearance, and then we were cleared for takeoff.

The flight began smoothly; I climbed through the clouds, reached the assigned altitude, and was turned north a few minutes later. Soon, we were back in the clouds—the layer was thicker than had been forecast. Oh well, maybe I wouldn't be able to learn any sign language for a while; you don't let a non-pilot steer in the clouds.

One of my former flight instructors was flying a bigger plane and heard me on frequency. He made a pilot report to Los Angeles Center, which I knew was intended for my ears: he had encountered a little light icing at my altitude, but it hadn't lasted long. Okay, I should be in good shape.

I continued flying through the clouds, and a little ice began forming on the wingtips. It wasn't much— not enough to alter the shape of the airfoil—but it was enough to get my attention. I glanced at my en route chart and verified that I was just a few miles from where the minimum en route altitude (MEA) was lower than the altitude I was currently flying. I called ATC to request the lower altitude as soon as possible—the temperature would be above freezing there. The controller acknowledged my request.

Then something happened that shouldn't—something that every pilot is trained to expect at any time but hopes never occurs, especially during flight in instrument conditions. The engine stopped.

The procedure for engine failure is to lower the nose to an attitude that allows the plane to fly at best glide speed, which gives the most distance for altitude lost. Decide where to land, or at least stop going toward an inhospitable site. Go through the checklist of items to check or change.

None of this takes more than seconds. At the same time, I called ATC and reported my engine out and said that I was descending. I told them that I could see some thin breaks in the clouds off to the side and would head in that direction. While I was talking, I changed to another fuel tank, and the engine came back to life.

Why didn't I change tanks at once? After all, that plane has four tanks.

The reason I didn't immediately change tanks is I knew I had lots of fuel in the one I was using. Only later did I learn that there was a defect in the fuel system. There had been several reports of this exact problem happening to this model of plane, but it took a while for the information to be shared by the FAA.

When the engine recovered, I reported in to Los Angeles Center and asked to climb back to the lower altitude I'd requested. That was granted. Another good thing: as I'd descended, the ice had melted. Since I never had to go back to my higher cruise altitude with its colder temperature, the ice never returned.

And then the communication radios quit! I'm not sure why; I wonder if the melted ice somehow got into the system. Whatever the cause, you can see how important it is to have a good IFR clearance to the destination. I did, and I flew in the clouds all the way to Modesto, using the standard IFR lost communications procedures of following the clearance you had received or had been told to expect.

I emerged out of the clouds while on the ILS approach. Just as I was about to land, the radios recovered and I heard, "645, cleared to land."

I acknowledged the clearance, landed, and contacted Ground Control. A friendly voice told me where to park and commented, "You've had quite a trip. Good job."

It's nice to know the system works well; the controllers from each sector I'd transited had kept me on radar and reported the situation to the next.

What of my family during all this? They were fine. My husband knew the engine had stopped and that we were in the clouds with ice on our wings. When I first became a pilot, he chose not to become one himself because "pre-menopausal women don't have heart attacks." He was a cardiologist and knew the statistics. He also decided to trust me because he wasn't really interested in learning about aviation.

The children heard the change in sound when the engine stopped but reported later that they weren't worried, because I didn't sound fearful. They had become pretty seasoned passengers—they always had things along to keep them amused, or they went to sleep.

Even I wasn't exhausted by the whole ordeal, as I would have guessed. Instead, I was actually exhilarated. While there had been lots of problems, following the correct procedures solved them.

~~~~~~~~~~~~~~

I enjoyed flying for family trips. Once, I talked my husband into flying to Iowa two months in a row. The first trip was for my parents' 50th wedding anniversary. For the second trip, the destination was Webster City, Iowa, for our 20th high school reunion; we'd been in the same graduating class.

The flight took about ten hours, which we did in two or three days, there and back again. It would have been quicker and cheaper to take an airline flight, but it wouldn't have been as much fun.

I relished the idea of landing on the local runway, and it was a rush. I flew over the small town, checking out the golf course being used by classmates. Pretending that I needed to take a look at the landing strip, I made a low pass, followed by a full power climb, all six cylinders joining to create a delicious racket. Then I climbed back to pattern altitude and landed.

The trip back to Santa Barbara was fun, too, particularly going into Albuquerque. The city is bordered by high mountains, and I needed to begin my approach at 12,500 feet. The guy ahead of me was in a turbocharged but non-pressurized twin. He annoyed the controller by refusing to take off his oxygen mask momentarily while acknowledging his clearances; his transmissions were pretty garbled.

He was at the same altitude as I was. Oxygen is only required for pilots when flying for more than 30 minutes between 12,500 and 14,000 feet. Since I was there only briefly, I was speaking unimpeded.

Then the guy complained that he couldn't descend fast enough to make a straight-in approach, and so he was no longer number one to the airport. He was told to circle to lose his altitude.

I chuckled all the way to the ground as I accepted the straight-in landing approach, slowed a little to gear speed (which brought me quickly to flap speed), lost altitude quickly, and was on the ground in no time. That's my idea of a good time.

~~~~~~~~~~~~~~

I wasn't the only one who liked to have a little fun. One of the owners of the FBO where I based my plane was a highly skilled pilot named TC. When I was flying my Bonanza one day, we discovered we were both the same distance from the airport. Neither of us had passengers aboard, so he challenged me to a race.

I asked what kind of plane he was flying. It was an old Piper Seneca, a twin with about the same speed as my single. I agreed, and then TC stipulated that I couldn't add power. That was ok with me because I was fairly high, and I could maintain a good speed as I descended.

You're not really supposed to chitchat on the frequency, but this was many years ago, and it was a slow time of day, so the controllers got into it, too. When I reported the 45 for downwind, local control cleared me, "Bonanza 86 Tango, Santa Barbara Tower, Runway 15, cleared to land. And good luck."

Soon after, TC reported a straight-in final for 25. It was a different runway, but we had agreed that whoever cleared the runway first would win.

I touched down first, but then my engine decided to quit. Drat! I told the tower that I'd have to restart and would be off the frequency briefly. Since I had landed well away from the intersection of 15 and 25, this didn't cause any problem. (25 was the favored runway at that time because of the wind.)

The plane cooperated and allowed me to restart its engine quickly, and I managed to taxi off the runway just as TC touched down. Ground control gave me clearance to the ramp, adding, "Congratulations!"

~~~~~~~~~~~~~

Some aviators, mostly men but a few women, feel that you can hardly consider yourself a real pilot unless you fly taildraggers. Taildraggers are planes that have their third wheel at the back rather than the front. At rest, or slow taxi, the small tailwheel supports the back of the craft much lower than the larger main wheels do—it looks like the tail is dragging. Taildraggers are called conventional gear airplanes, although the tricycle arrangement is the one used in most modern airplanes. Read more about flying taildraggers in the online appendix: http://www.awomansplaceisinthecockpit.com/appendix

In the air, taildraggers fly like other planes. The difference becomes apparent in the fast taxi portion of flight: just before takeoff and right after landing, when the plane is just below flying speed. That part is challenging because the center of gravity is in another location in taildraggers. In the case of a tricycle gear airplane, if the pilot doesn't land with the wheels perfectly aligned with the runway, the plane rights itself with a "squeak, squeak," and nobody outside the plane even notices, because the center of gravity is forward of the main landing gear.

In a taildragger, the center of gravity is behind the main gear, so the results are quite different. If the landing is askew, the plane will still right itself, but unless the pilot is really on top of the situation, it does it by means of a 180-degree turn (or 170 or 195). Everyone sees it happening—the plane is suddenly going in the opposite direction from the pilot's intention.

Someone told me this, no doubt fictional, anecdote: "A pilot lands a little taildragger poorly and it spins around. The guy in the control tower asks, 'Three Foxtrot Tango, do you need assistance, or would you like me to play a little music?'"

I loved flying taildraggers. Even more, I loved flying the ones that were capable of aerobatics. I flew quite a few hours in several Citabria 7KCABs. This model features a fuel injection system rather than a carburetor, and an inverted oil system was fitted to the engine. All of these changes were made in order to allow for extended inverted flight, which wasn't possible in earlier Citabria models. Tom McKenna, who taught me to fly taildraggers and to perform aerobatics in his KCAB, loved to point out that Citabria spelled backwards is Airbatic.

There are lots of other airplanes capable of aerobatics, such as rolls and loops. The ones used by professional aerobatic pilots can be maneuvered through very demanding routines. On the other hand, some planes that are categorized as acrobatic are very limited. For example, if they don't have an inverted oil system, the engine stops after a short period of upside-down flight. Also, many don't have powerful enough engines to perform many aerobatic maneuvers.

My friend Tom Zegers, who flew KCABs quite a bit, asked me to go with him in an acrobatic Sundowner one day. The Sundowner is a 180-horsepower low-wing Beechcraft aircraft that is quite heavy. As Tom told friends several times after our flight, "Beth was very calm as I tried to make the plane do something it couldn't. She just said, 'Remember, Tom, this isn't a Citabria.'"

Chapter 6

Going Pro

Maurine Leonard, the FAA designated examiner, agreed to be my instructor for my Commercial ticket. I admired her and thought it would be fun to have an experienced female instructor. And it was. For the first lesson we flew the Bonanza; then she said that the remainder of the instruction could be in a simple plane that was less expensive to operate. So I flew a Piper Warrior, a 150-horsepower low-wing airplane.

I loved the Commercial training course. I had acquired enough experience that I felt confident in my ability to put a plane just where I wanted it. The certificate attests to a pilot's much more precise flying of familiar maneuvers, takeoffs, and landings learned for the private pilot certificate, as well as specific Commercial maneuvers such as lazy eights and chandelles. It's a good excuse to play with an airplane.

Once I was ready, Maurine suggested I fly with my friend Marilyn for the formality of three hours with another instructor. That way, Marilyn could do the recommendation and Maurine could do the checkride. I did, and we had fun, too.

The day of the checkride, I looked at Maurine, and she had turned back into the awe-inspiring FAA designee. I was very tense.

The test was not what I expected. I had understood that we would use only the simple airplane, but as we were preflighting it, Maurine noticed the Bonanza being towed. She asked me about that and I said it was just having a light replaced. She said that we would be flying it in about an hour and to make sure it was ready. Oh dear, I hadn't practiced maneuvers in my plane in a long time.

Nevertheless, after performing chandelles, lazy eights, and other maneuvers in a Warrior, I took off again, this time in the Bonanza. At the end of the flight, Maurine asked which I'd prefer to do, a short field or a soft field landing—that choice again.

I admitted that I'd never done a soft field landing in 86 Tango. She laughed and said that I still had the option. I asked what would happen if I attempted one and messed it up.

"Depends on how badly you mess it up."

So, of course, I chose the challenging soft field landing, which allows an airplane to touch down at a slower speed than usual by adding power, lowering the stall speed. Oh boy, how nicely a Bonanza will allow itself to be coaxed into a beautiful soft field landing. The stall warning seemed to blare for 30 seconds, although it couldn't have been that long.

I was so impressed with the Bonanza's capability that I performed another simulated soft field landing at the end of a pleasure flight with my husband and kids. Again the plane slowed and slowed, strident stall warning persisting, until I finally allowed the nose to lower.

As I taxied off the runway, I asked my family if anyone noticed if the stall horn was working. They all said no. It was a beautiful maneuver, wasted on folks anxious to get out of the little aircraft and start a vacation.

Of course, these were simulated soft field landings. If it were a real soft field, you'd never take off the power until tying down the airplane.

Most soft fields, which could be tall grass or mud, for example, don't lead to a paved taxiway. Chances are, you will need power to keep up momentum all the way to the parking place.

The soft field landing that completed my checkride was certainly a success. As Maurine wrote out my new temporary certificate, she asked me if I intended to go for the next rating: Certified Flight Instructor (CFI). I said no. I hadn't entertained the idea before.

She said she thought I would be a good instructor. When I thought about it, I realized that my only objection was that I didn't want to teach something I loved to unenthused pupils. I had done that when I was in college—I was a piano major, and I gave piano lessons. Very few of the young students I had were happy to practice. That wasn't fun. On the other hand, I had enjoyed my five years of teaching elementary grades in the public schools.

~~~~~~~~~~~~~~

And so I began studying again. At that time, I couldn't find a textbook with a complete course of study for the CFI certificate, and so I had to use the little booklet that listed the tasks that need to be demonstrated on the oral and flying portions of the flight test. Then I found reading materials on as many of those subjects as I could.

After I'd read them, I took the two written tests required for the rating. In those days, the CFI written exams were administered at regional FAA offices, so I flew to Van Nuys and asked for the CFI test. The woman in charge of giving the exams said that I'd need to take the Fundamentals of Instructing first. I knew that I wasn't required to take that test, since I had a teaching credential. But she couldn't be persuaded.

Knowing that I didn't need to sit for that one, I'd only read the applicable information once, months before. But I didn't want to waste the trip, so I took it anyway. It was pretty much common-sense educational psychology, with a few unique FAA opinions on teaching.

When I'd finished the short test after only 20 minutes, I asked for the other, longer test. At first, she refused, saying that there needed to be five hours available and there were only four left before the office closed. I pointed out that I'd just taken a three-hour test in 20 minutes and promised that I would stop if I hadn't finished the other one by closing time. It took me just under two hours to complete.

After that, it was on to the real stuff: how to convey to the student the subjects and skills required to become a pilot. I read all the articles and booklets I could borrow or buy and filled hefty scrapbooks with copies of all this information, including diagrams and Federal Aviation Regulations. I picked the brains of various instructors, choosing the person I thought would be most knowledgeable on each topic. When I flew my family to Sedona for a little vacation, I spent my time there ignoring the breathtaking scenery in favor of sticking my nose into a book. It was overkill, I know, but I wanted to come as close as possible to learning everything about being a flight instructor.

Then I practiced on people. I'd teach a ground lesson to someone who didn't know how to fly. I'd teach a commercial maneuver to a pilot who was a private pilot.

I taught every flight maneuver and information topic at least once. I also took a few formal lessons from experienced instructors. Then, when I thought I was ready, I talked the chief pilot at the school into signing me off for the test. Dave had his own minimum standards of what he needed to see me demonstrate before agreeing that I was ready. We did a couple of flights and went over some knowledge stuff, and then I was pronounced ready.

(Later, when I was teaching flight instructors, I outlined a course of study for my students, including their making scrapbooks like mine. One person just copied mine and, of course, didn't really know the material because I was the one who had done the research, not him. Eventually, there were printed textbooks containing most of this material—that made it easier for both the students and me.)

The Certified Flight Instructor checkride was the scariest because the FAA made no secret of the fact that their inspectors flunk a sizable proportion of applicants. I didn't stop to reason this out. I just prepared like crazy. If there was anything in any of my books that I didn't understand, I was relentless in my search to figure it out.

There was one small point related to an illustration that I couldn't comprehend. I asked several experienced flight instructors. The answer tended to be that I'd never get asked about that. My reaction was that if there were a point that I didn't get, I'd definitely be asked about it. Finally, I discovered that the illustrations on the page were mislabeled; I'd been looking at the wrong one.

When the time came for my checkride, I learned that I had been assigned the toughest FAA guy at the Van Nuys office. He was known for intimidating people and failing a lot of applicants. I thought that the only advantage I might have was that I was using my Bonanza, and Mr. P. was a Beech fan.

I flew to Van Nuys, went to the district office, and took a seat among other nervous applicants, all men. A few minutes later, Mr. P. appeared. He scowled and asked me if I was the young lady applying for a flight instructor certificate. A smart retort hurtled out of my mouth: "As opposed to all these other young ladies?"

He frowned a few more seconds and then laughed.

I thought I'd blown it then. I didn't realize until later that my not being cowed by Mr. P. was probably an asset. Flight instructors must be in charge, and they will face intimidating students. The FAA was looking for confidence as well as skill.

The oral portion went well. I really knew my stuff and I had experience as a schoolteacher. Teaching one thing is similar to teaching another. Also, I was in my early thirties, rather than eighteen, the scarily young age at which one can become a flight instructor.

The flight test was a breeze. I knew my airplane and flew it well. After a while, Mr. P. took the controls and asked me to critique him, then showed me a few techniques that he favored. He did this for quite awhile, obviously enjoying the plane. I knew that I had passed then, although I'd probably passed early in the oral, assuming that I could handle the aircraft.

I saw Mr. P. many times in the following years. He remembered me, partly because women flight instructors are fairly rare. Also, I think he liked and respected me.

~~~~~~~~~~~~

I had hoped to be hired as a flight instructor by the flight school where I learned to fly, but I wasn't. The head of the company wanted me, but the chief flight instructor didn't. Maurine, the FAA designee who had suggested that I become an instructor, asked the chief if he was afraid he couldn't control me. He didn't answer.

I'd like to think it was just because I wanted to work part time, although I wasn't told that.

I freelanced for a while. There was a loosely organized flying club that gave me the opportunity to find students and use their airplanes. Also, I was able to give instruction to members of the Santa Barbara Flying Club in their club planes.

Freelancing with the clubs was a bad idea. New instructors need the support of experienced teachers, and flying clubs tend to be lacking in various areas, such a good maintenance program. So I got a job at Santa Barbara Aviation as a Beech Aero Club instructor.

~~~~~~~~~~~~

I was hired by Cliff Beeler, the head of the newly formed Beech Aero Club. He was also the salesman who had demonstrated a brand new Bonanza to me a few years prior. I would be the primary flight instructor or "pro," as I learned I should be called—as in "golf pro."

Beechcraft had decided to promote sales of their airplanes by sprinkling identical Beech Aero Clubs across the United States. The ideas was to teach people how to fly in a little Beech Sport or Sun-downer, encourage them to buy an airplane, and let brand loyalty prompt the sales of Bonanzas, Barons, and Dukes.

The BAC at Van Nuys Airport was built to Beech's specifications, and all others were to be just like it. This didn't happen. The individual Beechcraft dealers opted not to spend the money to create exact copies. Instead, the BACs tended to be housed in existing hangars and office spaces. We had part of a large WWII hangar at Santa Barbara Airport.

There was a myriad of lists and forms and definitions and so forth—much more paperwork than made sense in an efficient oper-ation, so once we got going, we ignored a lot of it. And I never had to be called a pro.

Cliff was a former U2 pilot with some great stories. He attracted pilots and would-be pilots with his cigar smoking monologues. It was very entertaining, but I was glad when California decided to protect us from smoke-filled rooms.

Rather than presenting the Beech Aero Club as an exclusive place to belong, Santa Barbara Aviation switched to promoting it as a cost-saving option for learning to fly. It really wasn't. Members got a dis-count on plane rentals and instructors' fees, but club membership came at a price. Unless a person flew very often, the costs evened out.

However, there were rewards for joining the club. First, there was a place to hang out. Pilots and students tend to love spending time at the airport. We created events to attract members and prospective members. There are lots of fun excuses to do a group fly-in to another airport, and sometimes we would make our own event.

Sometimes we would just have a few planes fly to Santa Maria for lunch. A student on a solo cross-country, an instructor with a student learning how to navigate, my multi-engine student proudly demon-strating his impressive takeoff after lunch, a few pilots in rented or owned planes—all indulging in the $100 hamburger, as a flight to have lunch was often called because of the expenses to operate the airplane.

Sometimes, several planeloads would fly to Sedona, AZ, for a weekend, negotiating the airport on the hill and soaking up the beautiful red rocks. Other times, we flew in to Sunriver, Oregon, a fly-in resort where we rode bikes, fished, swam, and partied. All the guests flew there, and there were few cars. The fly-in resort provided bikes. We had lots of fun places to go.

Besides trips, we also hosted poker runs and flour-bombing contests. Poker runs are an excuse to fly to several nearby airports, picking up a playing card at each one. At the end of the day, the best hand wins.

Flour-bombing involves flying about 50 feet over a nearly deserted runway which has been marked with an x. A baggie filled with baking flour is tossed out of each plane; whoever comes closest to hitting the x is the winner.

One favorite place to do this was New Cuyama, a very quiet landing strip within easy flying distance. It always had a very few airplanes tied down there but usually no sign of other activity. We had a bull's-eye painted on the runway, and it was the target. Each entrant would fly over the runway at 50 feet above ground level (AGL) and toss out their bags, one per circuit.

New Cuyama was also a good place for spot landing contests. Everybody loved watching the attempts and judging who got closest. There were not official communications at the airport, but we used our planes' communications radios and handheld transceivers to coordinate.

The first time I was involved in a spot landing contest was at the end of a local treasure hunt in which several entrants had tied. I was in the right seat while Shy flew the plane. She was reluctant to try to win the landing contest and said I should do it. As a brand new private pilot, I knew there was no way I could land from the right seat, so I told her I'd talk her through it.

She landed right on the spot. That was when I knew that it was much easier to teach than to do!

Spot landings involve reducing power to idle abeam the numbers and then adjusting the flight path using attitude, flaps, and leg length to land just at the designated spot. You can't land before the spot, and you can't add power.

That is, you can't add power unless you are going to crash—then you should add power and forfeit the contest.

The girlfriend of the chief pilot at Apollo had lost her husband in a spot landing contest. It shouldn't have happened; it occurred because he followed the rules at the expense of safety. So when I organized events for groups of pilots, my rule was that a student could compete only with an instructor in the right seat. A private pilot also needed a co-pilot: either a commercial pilot with a right seat checkout or an instructor. That took care of the potential for poor judgment by novice competitors.

Once, a bunch of planes made the Beech Aero Club trip to Apple Valley for a spot landing competition. We all had fun on the cross-country to the event, the picnic lunch, and meeting the host group, another BAC. For the contest, there were several categories: students, with an instructor aboard; private pilots, also with a professional in the right seat; and holders of commercial certificates.

Unfortunately, it was quite a warm day, which exacerbated the effects of the altitude. (Apple Valley Airport sits at 3062 feet above sea level.) But that provided a good learning opportunity for people who had little experience with high density altitude, and they handled it much better by the time they made their third landings.

Sometimes, we would rent one room at the nearby motel so that we could use their swimming pool. The owners were fine with that, and occasionally we even all got rooms and stayed the night so that we could have a little party.

Even when there wasn't an organized event, a lot of airports have decent restaurants, and sometimes we'd just fly to another airport for lunch. We'd take any good excuse to make a short flight and have some fun.

In the winter, ski trips were a favorite club activity. We'd load up some Bonanzas and Duchesses and head for Mammoth or Tahoe. A couple of days on the slopes followed by getting together for dinner in the evenings made for a busy weekend.

One weekend, we flew to western Arizona to see the newly imported and installed London Bridge. Most any excuse was good enough to take a trip with several other planeloads of folks.

~~~~~~~~~~~~~~

When Cliff Beeler hired me as the pro at the Santa Barbara Aviation BAC, there was one person who didn't interview me: Pete, the chief pilot of Santa Barbara Aviation. Pete was a tough old guy with tons of hours of experience, and he wasn't expecting to welcome me.

At first, I wasn't very busy, just doing an occasional checkout in a 150-horsepower Sport or a 180-horsepower Sundowner. However, as the fledgling Beech Aero Club picked up steam, student pilots decided to join the club in order to have a friendly place to hangar fly. In order to be able to instruct using the rules of FAR 141, which are strict but allow for fewer hours of flight experience for a pilot who achieves the required proficiency for a rating, I needed to have a standardization flight with Pete.

We had scheduled this checkout a few times, but each time, it had been cancelled because some other task demanded Pete's time. A quick flight to the Channel Islands, a former SBA pilot came to see him— anything to thwart me, I thought. So when I arrived at the FBO to see a dense layer of fog, I expected another cancellation, because the flight would require an IFR departure and approach, as well as takeoffs and landings at another airport.

Surprise! Pete thought it was a great day to go. It didn't occur to me that the weather conditions would let Pete see how I handled a lot of things. He was correct in deciding it was a good day.

My skills were good, and the instrument departure went well. We did some airwork on the way to Santa Ynez. I did a couple of touch and goes; then I was directed to do a short field landing on the next circuit.

Hmm, I knew that Pete had been a navy pilot and was a proponent of the old method of coming in with a lot of power and then chopping the power right over the chosen landing spot. Or, as he told students, "Take off all the power when you're at a height from which you could jump." I hated that technique. It made for bone-rattling arrivals. It was very inelegant. It worked, but I thought it was unprofessional.

Since he didn't specify the technique I was to use, I did my usual short field landing. I touched down smoothly a few inches past the target spot and braked quickly.

Pete growled and announced that he would demonstrate his technique. As expected, we arrived roughly and suddenly. He looked at me as if for admiration, until I pointed out that I had set the little Sport down a bit closer to the target spot. Again, I was rewarded with a growl, but he didn't disagree. After I executed a nice instrument approach into Santa Barbara, I was given my FAR 141 authorization.

Because I was an owner of a Bonanza and had flown it a lot, Pete decided he'd better give me a company checkout in that type of airplane, too, although it wasn't used for flight training. There were several Bonanzas on the flight line, but they were rented to pilots for cross-country flights.

Again it was a nasty day, this time because of really gusty wind. We flew west of the airport for some airwork, and that was easy. I really knew Bonanzas, and at altitude, it wasn't particularly bumpy. I'd always wanted to fly an aerobatic Bonanza but had been advised to not buy one if it would be a leaseback plane, because it would be just asking for someone who didn't know what he was doing to have a terrible result to an attempt at becoming a show pilot. I was still tempted until I learned that the insurance would be astronomically higher in price because of this very risk.

I did want to try a roll; I knew Pete liked to show off with them sometimes. My own plane was a v-tail, which didn't lend itself to such maneuvers, but we were doing the checkflight in a straight-tail plane. When I requested to try one, Pete was agreeable. Oh my, it was much more interesting with all those 285 horses than in my previous experiences with lighter, less powerful planes.

Then we went back to the traffic pattern. The wind had gotten even more squirrelly, and my first approach was acceptable but not right on. Pete muttered something, and so I initiated a go-around and came back, determined to make a pretty approach and landing. I did. I started to retract the flaps and take off again, but I heard Pete tell the tower that it would be a full stop. We taxied back to the tiedown area, and he actually told me I had done a good job.

So I was only mildly surprised when Pete asked me to come into his office one day and told me that he wanted me to do some retraining with a known hotshot pilot who had gotten cited by the FAA. I didn't know "Jeff" except by reputation, and I wondered how big a challenge this assignment would be.

I was immediately relieved when Jeff came for his first appointment. I asked him to tell me what had happened, and he was very quiet and apologetic about it. He said he loved flying and he would do whatever needed to be done to have his privileges reinstated. He said he had heard I was an expert in Bonanzas and he hoped to learn a lot. We came up with an extensive plan of ground and flight instruction, and we both enjoyed the project. We agreed on overkill, and we discussed all the performance charts and systems. We flew all the possible maneuvers usually required on a thorough checkout and then some.

Jeff felt well prepared and confident. We discussed demeanor, just in case he reacted differently with a male inspector. He passed with flying colors, and I was happy with the complimentary debriefing the examiner passed on to me.

After that, word got around. People started asking for me when they were due for a Biennial Flight Review or an insurance-mandated recurrence flight in a Bonanza. That was fun.

One man was an airline pilot who commuted to work at LAX, where he was based, every time he was scheduled for a flight. He was fairly senior at the base, so he was able to fly few, long trips, which meant that the commute wasn't so bad. Seldom is there weather in the area that would preclude being able to fly rather than drive. He had his own Bonanza, an older one. We did all the standard maneuvers and threw in a few instrument procedures.

I asked him how long it had been since he had done an emergency gear extension. I was very surprised to learn that he had never done that. I told him we really should do it. That way, in case he ever needed to do it for real, he would be familiar with the feel.

The procedure involves 51 rotations of a hand crank, which gets harder to do as it progresses. It's not such a chore if you can do it from the back seat, but likely you will be by yourself, so that won't be an option.

I was sympathetic to the effort required, but he was a reasonably big guy, and I'd done it a couple times. Leverage matters, and I'm 5'5". So, no, I wasn't all that sorry for him. He was happy to know what to expect if he ever needed the backup.

Chapter 7

Working as an Instructor

Being a flight instructor provides a lot of opportunities for fun, but of course the majority of the time it involves teaching people how to fly, doing aircraft checkouts and biennial flight reviews, as well as instructing applicants for advanced ratings. In order to do the latter, the instructor must hold the appropriate Flight Instructor ratings such as instrument and multiengine.

If a person has some instructing experience, earning an instrument flight instructor rating is much easier than the initial certified flight instructor certificate. When I got mine, I didn't have a whole lot of hours, but I had enough that I didn't have to think about the mechanics of instructing. It had become comfortable. I just needed to become familiar with teaching the instrument maneuvers.

When I had worked on my CFI, the most complicated part was flying the maneuvers from the right seat and describing what I was doing. This time, that wasn't so hard because, I had more experience in the right seat and talking isn't a weak point of mine.

My friend Marilyn's husband offered to be my guinea pig. Joel was a private pilot. He enjoyed flying the plane, even if it was under a hood, and he had the appropriate proficiency as would an actual instrument student. This allowed me to demonstrate and then talk him through maneuvers and also to see what errors a typical student would make and how to correct them.

When It came time for my Instrument Flight Instructor checkride, the good news was that I was assigned the FAA examiner who was supposed to be the best, fairest, and easiest to get along with. The bad news was that he called me a couple days prior and said that he had some FAA thing that he had to do in the afternoon the day of my scheduled ride. I told him it wouldn't take all day, that he'd either like my style or hate it. He thought that was funny and agreed to keep the date. I really didn't want to wait another three weeks or so for a reschedule.

Once more, I had my single yoke, which allows the right seat occupant a lot of leg room, swapped for a dual, which allows both front seat pilots access to all the controls except the brakes. And off I went to Van Nuys again. We got along great and everything went fine until I got my clearance for the ILS to Burbank. I was told to maintain 80 knots. A very slow speed for a Bonanza. I would much rather use 140 or 120, even 160 if descending. Less time to make errors!

I asked the controller why so slow and he said that I was following a Cessna 150. Oh. The 150 couldn't do much more than 80 knots. There's no passing allowed on instrument approaches. However, I did pass the checkride.

~~~~~~~~~~~~~

I usually enjoyed teaching instrument students. Most of them understood what was involved and were able to learn the techniques and concepts with reasonable effort. Occasionally, there would be one that just couldn't handle the tasks which differ significantly from VFR maneuvers. I tried various methods to make things make sense. For example, I would have a person fly without a hood sometimes so that he/she could see the relationship to the navigational station when flying holding patterns, for example.

I learned and invented some helpful techniques for helping people understand a few of the tricky procedures such as navigating with the old ADF, an imprecise radio/ground gadget seldom used anymore. Sometimes an instrument instructor candidate would demonstrate one of these to the FAA examiner conducting the checkride and would hear, "Oh, you know Beth."

~~~~~~~~~~~~~~

I remember some of my students very well, at least the ones whom I shepherded through an entire certificate or rating. I also remember some of the ones with whom I flew only a few times.

It was fun flying with "Doug," a psychiatrist. He was smart and funny. He was doing something just for the joy of it; I don't know if he intended to complete his private pilot course. One thing that I have never forgotten about him is that he completely lost his perspective when it came to analyzing his own performance. We were in the touch and go stage, perfecting landings. You can practice all the elements of the approach and landing regime at altitude, but when it comes down to the last 10 feet or so, it isn't the same at altitude. You really need to be next to the ground, partly because ground effect comes into play, but also because doing it at 3000 feet just doesn't have the same effect as being right above that hard surface.

One day, after about an hour of working on landings, I said that we would make the next one a full stop. Doug said he wanted to keep going. I insisted. After landing, he said he was really tired and he supposed I was, too. I laughed and suggested that he think about why I wasn't later.

The two most outstanding private pilot students I ever had were Randy and Kyle.

Randy was very talented. I don't think he had the benefit of any prior flying experience, but he was the perfect raw material: about 18, male, wanting desperately to fly, and he had a job at the airport, fueling airplanes. The position allowed him to absorb the atmosphere and also to learn radio communications while working, which let him think about flying, not talking, during lessons.

Randy soloed in six hours; he was very proud but confessed that he had spent as much time as possible going along on all kinds of flights whenever a pilot let himself be talked into it. He seemed surprised that I didn't consider this to be cheating.

One not-so-good trait about Randy, not an unusual thing in young men under the age of about 25, was his supreme confidence. This in a kid who slept in a shed at the airport for lack of funds. Randy really wanted to earn his private in 35 hours, the minimum allowable in an FAA approved flight school. (It was 40 in non-approved schools.)

I was willing to try to meet his goal, but I wasn't willing to turn out a young, bold, dangerous pilot. I always assumed that the flight after which I signed someone off for a checkride would be the last one the student would fly with me—no cleaning up any rough spots after the certification.

Santa Barbara has a lot of days when there is a thin marine layer, otherwise known as a fog bank, right at the edge of the active runway. Sometimes we make instrument departures, but other times we can maintain legal separation from the clouds with just a regular takeoff. This was a day when I could see that we would come close to entering the clouds, so I got an instrument clearance.

Naturally, Randy wanted to fly the instrument departure himself, which isn't unusual. Students are allowed to do this if their instructor is pilot-in-command. However, Randy felt that he could accomplish the departure without my coaching. I agreed that he could attempt it.

Surprised that I was sitting with my hands in my lap (it doesn't take long to move them), Randy got a little nervous and held the plane on the runway longer than necessary. Therefore, instead of coming close to the clouds, his technique put him right into the marine layer.

I kept my mouth shut and watched him falter a little, but it was a very thin layer and we were on top in seconds. Had I wanted to reassure him, I would have directed his attention to where the land was visible, which would correct his untrained reaction... But I wanted this to be a big learning experience, and so as soon as I could legally cancel the clearance, I made him put on a hood and directed him to perform some unusual attitudes. Although he was still feeling wobbly, he did quite well; this wasn't a new maneuver to him, just a new situation.

And then, I announced that the engine had just failed as I retarded the throttle. The kid was incredible. He set up perfectly for an emergency landing. Then we went back to the airport for a full stop. This all took less than half an hour.

He did learn from this; he was chastened. Somewhat. I don't think that was the day that he started calling himself my number-one student, but he did later sign the notes he sometimes sent me that way.

That wasn't the only time over-confidence got Randy. Another time, we were going on our first dual cross-country; I think the goal was San Luis Obispo. Usually, students spend a few hours of ground instruction before they even start planning their first trip. However, Randy announced that he had studied thoroughly and would have the venture planned perfectly, so we could just preflight and go. I wasn't charging Randy for my time, so that wasn't the reason for this.

In addition, to save money, Randy had talked Bob the tower controller into loaning him his Cessna 150 for the trip. Randy would only have to pay for fuel and oil rather than a rental fee. This was a high-winged airplane rather than the low-wing we had flown up until then.

I agreed because he was adaptable, and for the cross-country it really didn't matter. Always pushing, Randy asked that I help him a bit with the landing when we came back, in case Bob was watching—as if I wouldn't have thought of the fact that he would need some coaching.

The time came to go and I asked to see his plan. He had only one sheet of paper, which he assured me was a distillation of his extensive planning project. Certain that his calculations were perfect, he suggested that I allow him to prove himself in the air. I agreed, although I assumed that this would cost him time and money—which it did.

After takeoff, we headed for Gaviota VOR, a nearby navigation facility. We had done this on previous flights because it is on the way to nearby Santa Ynez Airport, being situated on the low point of a mountain pass. I did a lot of landing practice there with students who worked at the Santa Barbara Airport so that their friends wouldn't be watching.

After passing Gaviota, Randy proudly intercepted his planned new course, which headed us directly toward Vandenberg Air Force Base. I let him fly his route until it needed to be aborted before we entered military airspace. We could see the wrong airport ahead of us and I asked him where we were. He announced that it was Santa Maria, which he had intended to fly over.

The two airports do have a somewhat similar appearance. So many students make the mistake of approaching Vandenberg that when they call Santa Maria Tower for landing instructions and the controller doesn't see them, he will assume that they are near Vandenberg and turn them away while asking them to describe the aerodrome. The error usually arises when someone fails to fly his course and subconsciously heads away from the mountains.

But Randy had actually planned his heading to Vandenberg. Oh, yes, he had drawn the line on the sectional correctly. But then, using his own shortcut, he had figured a heading that was too far west. His mistake was subtracting the variation from the magnetic course rather than the true course. Magnetic course is the result of subtracting variation from true course. Since there is about 15° of variation in that area, this produced a significantly different course from the one leading to Santa Maria.

My suggestion that we go back to Santa Barbara produced consternation. Couldn't we please just go to Santa Maria? I agreed because using the sectional to find it was a good exercise in lost procedures.

He did a good job of finding the airport and wanted to land, but he didn't have the tower frequency. He didn't have it because he had skipped the study of the fine points of the sectional, so he didn't know where it would be listed. He was completely unaware of the fact that I had tuned in Santa Maria Tower when we turned away from Vandenberg. Student pilots have tunnel hearing.

When he gave up on finding the frequency, I showed him where it was on the chart and showed him that it was already tuned in. Naturally, he wanted to land, but I refused. He didn't really need an extra landing in a plane for which he hadn't learned the procedures.

So he flew us back to Santa Barbara, sadder and wiser. Oh, yes, I helped him achieve a pretty landing, just in case anyone was watching.

~~~~~~~~~~~~~~

Kyle was another very talented student. He had the advantage of having parents (or at least a mother) who flew, so he was accustomed to the airport. Another airplane fueler, he was able to spend as much time as he liked soaking up the atmosphere.

I soloed Kyle after just six hours of flight instruction. I kept the lessons short for the talented kids who mastered maneuvers fast and for keeps. The day I soloed him, I called the tower and asked for a full stop after just a couple of trips around the pattern. Kyle looked at me in disappointment as he taxied off the runway and asked why we had to stop. I said, "I'm going to solo you. Aren't you ready?"

The answer: "Yes, but I didn't think you knew it."

And he performed three nearly perfect takeoffs and landings.

Kyle was a dream student in pretty much all regards. When I had determined that he easily met the private pilot standards, I began the paperwork, which included adding up his hours. He had the required solo hours but needed three more dual instruction hours. When I say this is unusual, I mean it. And I'm not an easy instructor. My students always greatly exceeded the minimum skill level.

So we spent the next three hours working on challenging commercial maneuvers, chandelles, lazy eights, and pylon eights, which he learned easily. Needless to say, he soared through his checkride with flying colors.

Kyle was also my student for his Certified Flight Instructor preparation. He excelled there, too. When we were practicing having him teach a student to land, I made a number of landings that included typical student errors, and he critiqued them well. On the last landing, I followed his instructions, which had improved because of what he had learned on the previous ones: "Take off a little power. Lower the nose. There, that's the right attitude. Are you trimmed? Hold it off, hold it off, hold it off….great! Great landing!"

I looked over at Kyle in the right seat and was about to ask if that "great, great" comment wasn't a bit effusive, but I stifled the question when I realized that I was probably hearing my own words.

He was practicing the imprecise art of talking students through the last phase of a flight. It's hard to learn to land, and it's also hard to teach someone else to land, until you've done each many, many times. There's so much going on and each landing is different—wind, weight of plane and contents, etc. It takes about five minutes to fly the pattern and only seconds to complete the trickiest part. All the rest of the pattern can be practiced bit by bit at altitude, repeating the segments over and over. But although we simulate landings by completing the approach with a stall followed by a recovery, there is always safe air under us. Not so at the airport. What is always under us is hard, unforgiving concrete or asphalt. It takes a lot of practice to tell just where it is and when to touch it.

Flying came easy for Kyle but years later when he began working for an airline, he visited me and told me that he had trouble transitioning to the Boeing 737 he was assigned. My reply was "Good."

He looked at me in astonishment and then ventured that his mother had said the same thing.

~~~~~~~~~~~~~~

I hate to categorize people, but it is often possible to predict students' behavior by knowing their occupation.

Engineers crave exact measurements. Just how much rudder pressure is required for a given situation? There is no precise answer; whatever is required to achieve the result. It depends on wind, weight of the plane (which varies according to how much fuel it is carrying and how much the second person in the plane weighs), airspeed, and the angle of bank if turning.

Attorneys don't get excited when they solo. At least, they don't display the elation common to first soloists. And they won't admit that the flight was special, just another step in achieving the main goal.

College students haven't gotten much respect yet, so they are receptive of critiques. They don't perceive coaching as insults.

Successful businessmen do. They hate to be told that their performance is faulty.

And so on.

When I was teaching the certified flight instructor course, I used these categories to get my students to realize that they couldn't present information and maneuvers to all their potential students in the same way.

One of the things they would practice was explaining things to me and then flying with me as the student. I would tell them who I was: a 60-year-old successful businessman, a cocky teenager, or a homemaker who knew nothing about aerodynamics. The last category was hardest for them because that was kind of who I had been when I learned to fly, and they couldn't picture that. They also didn't want to insult me.

It's a real category, though. There were quite a few women with no previous scientific or aviation background who wanted to fly. Few of them had burning desires to become a pilot; they were taking the training just to see what it was like or because their husbands wanted them to.

The few who did have a real interest in becoming pilots had no more difficulty in learning than the men. It was the others that could be a challenge. The male instructors would often express their frustration and then ask me to do a flight with these women who progressed so slowly. It was easier for me than for them to tell a passive student that I was happy to fly her around, but that it wouldn't do much to make a pilot of her.

When women would tell me that they couldn't climb up on the stool to check the quantity of fuel in the wing tank of a high-wing airplane because of how they were dressed, I started wearing dresses and high heels to work. Then I could say, "If I can do it, so can you." And after we got into the airplane, I would take off my heels and toss them behind the front seats.

As the years went by and we had more young women wanting to become airline pilots than bored housewives, the difference between teaching a man and a woman became smaller. I was very happy to see that change. I was very proud of our excellent women students.

~~~~~~~~~~~~~~

My first years as a flight instructor were based at an airport without local radar. This would cause any flight under instrument conditions to take a lot more time than would be the case if there were radar available. Because of the airport being just inside the Pacific Ocean coastline, there were many, many days when the only way in and out of the airport was with an IFR procedure. And any flight on an IFR day would have to begin and end with an instrument clearance. The beginning portion didn't require much extra time; you just had to take your turn, waiting until the preceding flight reported on top and canceling IFR. This didn't take long because usually the tops of the clouds were at about two to three thousand feet.

However, the return to the airport could be time consuming. So as soon as we took off, climbed through the marine layer, and reported on top and canceling IFR, we would request an approach. The usual reply would be to announce that there would be about an hour's wait. There were always planes waiting for the approach and it was first-come-first-served. The one exception was the scheduled airline flights; they got priority.

Although my student might be a very early student, certainly not ready for IFR procedures, we worked around the situation. Approach control would send us to a particular point, an intersection of two VOR radials, where we would have an assigned altitude and would presumably be flying holding patterns until we were cleared to the next intersection. There, we would be expected to be conducting more holding patterns. And so on. However, since we were in the clear, on top of the clouds, we just used our assigned airspace to practice whatever maneuvers were appropriate for the particular student's progress.

With each new clearance, a new "expect further clearance" time would be issued. Each clearance required a read back to ATC, so there was a lot of chatter on the frequency. When we were assigned the last intersection before receiving our actual approach clearance, we would be given a new, lower altitude each time the people ahead of us made a descent. In clear air, on top, the holding patterns were arranged at 500-foot intervals, vertically. When the first guy in line landed, the next one would be allowed inbound from the "Final Approach Fix," a point created by an intersection of two navigation station radials or a marker beacon which beeped when crossed. Then the one behind him would be cleared toward the final approach fix, and so on. And we'd all get a lower altitude and an updated "Expect Approach Clearance" time.

All of this complicated stuff was further complicated by the fact that the different planes had different approach speeds. The controllers know the general range of possible speeds for each airplane type. Managing all of this was quite a skill for ATC folks. Now, if there is a radar failure, this procedure would still work, but controllers have long lost the ability to perform this juggling act.

The reason for the constantly changing Expect Approach Clearance times was that in case an airplane lost communication capability during the approach, it could use its most recent expect further clearance time to begin the approach. This happened rarely but I witnessed a few and actually used this myself a couple of times.

It was interesting when it happened to someone else. Everyone in the queue became aware of the situation because the controller would let us know and would ask one of the local professional pilots he recognized to monitor, visually, the actions of the non-com plane. Then, if I was selected, I would tell the tower that the plane had begun flying inbound when the time was right. This time, those of us who were waiting in line didn't get to move to the next fix until the quiet plane was in sight, in case something went askew. It was an intricate system but it worked well.

Under this system, it usually took about an hour to get back to the airport—the length of a usual lesson. It worked and we all took it for granted. If our flight took us away from the local area, we flew away and then when we came back, either the field had become VFR or we were worked into the queue for an instrument approach. A lot of things can be taught to a primary student while doing holding patterns: descents, changes in airspeed, IFR basic maneuvers, etc. We spent most of the time above the fog layer and just a few minutes actually in the clouds.

Eventually, Santa Barbara got radar. We knew that it was coming, but it was a surprise one day when I was flying with a student, having requested an IFR approach and been given the usual clearance for one of the fixes along the slow, non radar route to an ILS approach. We were in the vicinity of the fix, practicing slow flight when a familiar voice came on the frequency saying, "We can see you, Beth!"

The approach controllers were practicing with their new radar screens. Although they were still using the old procedures, they could now follow our track. I replied, "Roger." And then our slow flight practice moved to a tighter adherence to the holding pattern track.

I wondered how this new regime would work for lessons on cloudy days. But, of course, it made things considerably easier once the radar was fully commissioned. We'd do an IFR departure, conduct of a normal lesson on top or away from the local area, and then receive a quick clearance for an IFR approach. Now that the controllers could see the planes, they could vector (give each plane individual directions to fly) everyone efficiently and things moved smoothly and quickly.

Still, it was with some regret that we witnessed the changes to ATC. It became less personal. Even the names of the intersections lost their character when they were all renamed. All got five letter "pronounceable" designations. And so the local color names of intersections around coastal Santa Barbara went from Halibut to Habit; from Goleta, for the town surrounding the airport, to Golet; from Naples, a tiny town under the approach course, to Napps; and so on. Of course, when we flew in other areas we didn't remember the old local names and the new five letter combinations didn't seem odd. But I never forgot "Lobster" when I heard Lober.

~~~~~~~~~~~~~~

It is pretty easy to teach people how to fly. At the end of an introductory flight, I would say, "See how easy it is? You know how to fly now. You can climb, fly straight and level, turn and descend."

The wannabe pilot loved it and grinned.

The tough part isn't flying; it's landing.

I would teach a student almost every skill out in the practice area. Nearly everything can be taught at several thousand feet above the ground, even landing procedures. However, the tough part is the few seconds of flying right above the ground in the final stages of landing. That can't really be simulated at altitude because of both the psychological difference and the cushioning provided by ground effect.

There are methods to make it easier for the struggling student. I would have a student practice flying at slow speed the whole length of the runway to get used to the height. I would set the power, and on the last circuit, I would reduce it and we would land.

I would teach students the pictures that the changing runway makes. It always works, day or night.

I would fly the pattern so the person could rest and save his energy for the final leg and landing.

I would occasionally do the landing so she could observe what I did; I would talk through it to point out the steps. Also, this would help the person see the changing runway picture.

~~~~~~~~~~~~~

Teaching people to land isn't something to be taken lightly. When, after years of procrastination, I decided to end my marriage, I temporarily grounded myself from teaching.

My first student after I visited my lawyer was a woman of about my age with whom I got along well. I told her what had happened and that I felt it best to ground myself from flying with students in the learning to land phase for fear of being distracted at the most critical stages, near the ground. She was great about it and we went out for coffee and tea.

I continued this policy for a week or so, explaining the situation by phone and giving the students the option of flying with another instructor while my brain got used to the new situation. Divorce is unsettling even though I was the one that wanted it.

The day the announcement of my divorce appeared in the local newspaper, three days after I filed for dissolution of marriage, I took my rings off and went to work, wondering what the reaction would be. I knew that a lot of people read those items every morning. And, of course, the news travelled fast.

There were two distinct groups of comments. The first was made up of people who had never been married or were married for the first time. Those people either avoided conversation with me or made a brief comment of consolation. However, the other group overshadowed them. These were the people who had been divorced themselves; they heartily congratulated me. I was unprepared for this, but it cut through my nervousness and I was grateful. Although I had separated my work and home spheres, I guess people could tell I wasn't happily married anymore.

~~~~~~~~~~~~~~~

Just like people, all airplanes have their own personalities. Little planes that are rented to flight students develop very different characteristics. After all, they are tormented by many inelegant landings. They came from the factory perfectly rigged but the abuse to which they are subjected changes that.

The best thing about being a training airplane in an active flight school is that the planes fly every day. This is very good for their engines which don't like to sit on the ramp for weeks or months without exercise.

Flight instructors tend to have favorites. This varies from time to time, as each plane's condition is constantly altered by its novice flyers. Sometimes I'd choose a particular plane because it would stall cleanly or because another would have a tendency against coordination as it stalled. These characteristics would move from plane to plane as students' clumsy first attempts at landing rearranged the rigging.

One time, one of the Beechcraft Sports acquired a little shudder. It felt like the beginning of a full stall. We kept sending it to the maintenance shop, but they couldn't find anything wrong. Eventually it was discovered that a door wasn't closing cleanly; the air flow was interrupted, thus inducing the stall-like effect. After proper repairs, the plane became popular again.

At one point, I was working with an instrument student, "Gary." One day, when his own plane was in the shop for maintenance, I suggested that he fly one of the primary trainers instead. The Sports were very similar to his plane, a Sundowner, but they had less horsepower and consequently were cheaper to rent.

When Gary showed me the clipboard with his chosen rental, I nearly asked that he choose a different plane. I had been steering clear of 59Romeo because it had been running a little rough. But then I thought that if I wasn't willing to fly 59R, I should ground it. Besides, the symptom wasn't that pronounced.

When conducting an instrument flight, with the student "under the hood" (which means that the pupil's view is confined to the instrument panel and he can't see outside), the instructor controls just where the plane is located at all times. That day, I made sure that we were always within glide range of the airport. This was before our tower was equipped with radar, so we had a lot of freedom on where we conducted practice maneuvers.

I even kept Gary under the hood until we had turned final, because he had a tendency to fly his traffic pattern low with a lot of power if given the chance. I kept us high in case the engine should fail. That way, we still could glide to the runway.

The engine didn't fail in flight. However, it did as soon as we touched down.

I called the tower and explained that we would need a minute to get going again. Gary then began a normal restart. Normal, that is, until the engine burst into flames! I told Gary to get out, and he did.

I tried to extinguish the fire by cranking the engine, a standard technique, while the tower urged me to vacate the airplane and advised that the fire trucks were on their way.

I gave up. I wasn't able to contain the fire, so I got out, too. In my haste, I grabbed my purse but not my shoes. Oh, boy! That nice green grass surrounding the runways isn't grass! It has lots of prickles.

The fire department quickly extinguished the fire. By then, Airport Patrol was there, too. I asked the officer for a ride back to SBA, but he turned me down.

The disgusted firemen quickly offered Gary and me a ride in the big truck, which was more fun anyway. We were dropped at the maintenance facility just after the plane had arrived there under tow. The fire trucks followed the towed plane just in case—that's standard procedure.

Gary and I relived our experience, and I assured him that his procedures were completely correct. Then I walked over to the shop foreman. He had removed the cowling, leaving the engine exposed. I commented that Pete, the chief pilot, would likely kill me.

The mechanic said, "Not this time. Look." He pointed out a hose that had come unfastened.

In fact, I was rewarded by the FAA. The inspector in charge of investigating the event told me that he was classifying it as an incident, not an accident, because he felt that if someone else had been flying, the results might have been catastrophic. And since the fire was caused by a fluke, not a design flaw, it didn't merit the dissemination of information a flaw would have necessitated.

I was pleased. Filling out all the paperwork for an accident is very time consuming. And I felt good about the compliment from the crusty FAA guy with whom I had flown my CFI checkride. Plus, I didn't have to check the "yes" box on routine forms that asked if I had ever had an accident.

~~~~~~~~~~~~

Originally, I was the only Beech Aero Club active instructor. Cliff Beeler, who managed the club, had a flight instructor ticket, but he didn't teach anybody to fly. He demonstrated airplanes and flew on our club flights. Being a highly experienced military pilot including flying U2s, he also loved formation flight. He could move in next to another plane, including one I would be flying fairly often, and stay exactly the same distance away for any length of time. Our students and club private pilots loved that.

As the only active instructor for the club, I did checkouts for pilots who joined the club, and I taught members to fly. Eventually, this led to more instruction within the club. More people joined the club because they thought they'd enjoy the activities and being welcome to hang out with us. There was a lot of "hangar flying" every day: experienced pilots relating their adventures and novices enjoying the camaraderie. Many of our new members were people who wanted to learn to fly or earn a new rating.

After awhile, SBA realized that the BAC was generating its own students as well as airplane rentals. The way it was organized, financially, was that a pilot or family would buy one of a variety of categories of membership. For all except the social membership, pilots and students could rent airplanes at discounted rates. Of course, it was set up so that on average, the discounts were offset by the fees.

As more students opted for the BAC, two more instructors were added. Todd and Rick were nice, friendly guys. They were also good instructors. I did part of the training of both of them and could honestly vouch for their skills.

As we got busier, the atmosphere attracted more students. In addition, SBA made some radio commercials, advertising the club as offering discounted rates.

In the end, SBA management decided to disband the club because people were taking too much advantage of the price breaks. I was quite surprised; why didn't they just adjust the fee schedule? I did successfully argue that the existing members should be given a fair deal on ending their privileges.

Rick, Todd, and I just continued teaching people to fly at Santa Barbara Aviation. We still took trips occasionally, and I took over writing the company newsletter, which included news of coming events that we arranged.

Chapter 8

Fun and Adventures in Flying

S ome people prefer to leave their work behind when they go on vacation, but not me. Even on vacation, I loved flying or hanging around in airports.

The first time I vacationed in Hawaii was in April of 1976. We two couples spent a few days on Oahu and then moved on to Maui. Each of the four of us had different ideas of how we wanted to spend our days; naturally, I wanted to go to the airport. I discovered that the flight school had a Cherokee 140, the same kind of plane that I had used when I learned to fly. That made it easy, because it was one of the few types of aircraft that I knew thoroughly.

I booked a checkout, breezed through the paperwork, and answered the instructor's questions without any problem. We took off, did a few maneuvers, and then he pulled the engine. I went through all the procedures and chose a field. I remarked that since I wasn't familiar with the area, I perhaps hadn't chosen the best possibility, but he said that he didn't know of a better one. When it became obvious that I would make the field, he told me to go around and we headed back.

I had worried that I would forget the name of the airfield, Kahului, but while listening to other traffic, I discovered that most pilots just said Maui Tower. I contacted the tower for touch and goes, and we flew toward the runway.

The instructor, whose name I don't remember and whose writing in my logbook isn't clear, had warned me that mainland pilots were always unprepared for the customary 20 knots of headwind upon landing. He said that I should only use two notches of flaps, which would make it easier to manage a strong wind. He asked for a couple of landings, which I performed well despite the wind.

As we were flying downwind for the final touchdown, he challenged me to a short field landing at a spot much closer to the approach end than I had planned. He clearly didn't think I could do it. I said that I could, but I would need to use full flaps, which would give me more drag. He agreed to that. I used a severe slip and touched down right on the spot.

The instructor concurred that I had done well, but he said accusingly, "You've been flying taildraggers!" He reached that conclusion because often that kind of plane doesn't come with flaps and often a slip is used to lose altitude prior to landing. He was right; I had. But I would have known to slip even if I hadn't.

I was instrument rated, and this seemed to annoy the instructor. He had earned his CFI one of the last years that it was legal to do so without an instrument rating. And here I was, a woman no less, with a qualification he didn't have. He scowled at me and told me he didn't want me to fly into the clouds. I assured him that I had no intention of doing so. The plane's only navigation radio hadn't filled me with confidence in its accuracy when I'd glanced at it during our flight.

I was cleared to rent the plane. I signed up for the following day and returned to the airport to fly by myself, since none of my fellow vacationers wanted to go along. I looked forward to cruising around the island, checking out the sights. However, as I began my preflight, I found that the master switch had been left on by the previous pilot. It wasn't me; the plane had been flown since my checkout flight.

I hoped that a new battery could be installed, but that wasn't an option, so I sadly gave up on the idea of a Maui flight.

The next day, we went back to Oahu well before our departure from the islands. This allowed time for another flight. I asked to fly with an instructor, rather than do a checkout, because I had little time.

This time, I got a really nice, mellow guy. We had fun checking out Honolulu and the north shore. I had expected the Honolulu International Airport to be curt and busy like LAX. Not so. As we approached for landing, the controller gave me my traffic and then remarked that he couldn't see the plane he had mentioned. When I said I had it, he asked me if I could tell what kind of craft it was. I told him what it looked to be, and he thanked me and cleared me to land. An international airport with a tower with limited sight!

The other time I flew in Hawaii was several years later, again in Maui. By that time, I had been a flight instructor for a few years. I was there with a friend who had a private pilot license and wanted to try Hawaiian flying.

We went to the local FBO and found that they were now renting Cessna 152s, which my friend hadn't experienced before. We did the paperwork and discussed the characteristics of the little Cessna, and then came the flight checkout.

Of course, I couldn't go along because there are only two seats in this type of plane. Strangely enough, the instructor kept the flight very short, doing only one landing. I had told him not to worry about landings; I would make sure that later flights' touchdowns were kind to the aircraft.

I would never go along with such a request from a stranger if I were doing the checkout; the person receiving the training is the one who should be responsible for future flights. The instructor suggested that he check me out instead, but I turned down that idea, explaining that I had hundreds and hundreds of hours of experience in Cessna 152s.

I was obviously an instructor but unknown to the company. Actually, the owner offered me a job. That intrigued me briefly, but I declined. I realized that I'd never bother to go to work in the idyllic climate of Hawaii.

So we had a nice flight around the island—it's just as pretty from the air as on the ground. And I made sure the landing was light and graceful.

~~~~~~~~~~~~~~

In 1990, I travelled to Africa. One of my customers told me about the group of people, mostly from Santa Barbara, who were going. She suggested that I might like to go, too.

I did, and it was a perfect trip for me. We flew in lots of airplanes. First, we flew to London in a 747; then we flew to Johannesburg in another—a very long trip. After that, most of our moving from one country or site to another was done in small airplanes.

Since I was the only pilot in our group of about 20 or 30, I managed to score the right front seat in all the planes that had a single pilot. The smallest were Cessna 206s. That was fun! I have some terrific pictures from final approach to runways that were little better than cow fields. These guys flew without charts, and they flew low so we could better see the sights. It was a blast.

My friends in the back seats were sometimes apprehensive, but they saw my enjoyment and confidence and decided that all must be well. So I served a purpose.

On the way back to the USA, we retraced our steps. The flight from Johannesburg to London was very long again, droning on through the night. After several hours of intermittent dozing (I'm not a good airplane sleeper), I realized that we were descending. I asked a flight attendant what was happening. He told me that on an average of about once every two weeks, the winds required a fuel stop. This was that once.

By the time we landed, all of the passengers were looking out the windows. Here we were on an island off the west coast of Africa—an island which appeared to consist almost entirely of a very long runway.

And then Greg picked up a couple of us at LAX, and it was back to the reality of home and work. In fact, reality hit harshly: he told me that we lost an airplane while I was gone. He'd tried to call me, but I was totally out of phone reach in Botswana during that one- or two-day period, and then he decided not to ruin my vacation.

He and Christa handled it. This was during the summer, and they were both graduated from college but home for the summer. They took charge of the school while I was away.

~~~~~~~~~~~~~~

Pilots get to view many beautiful sights from above. One of my favorites is a glory. It resembles a rainbow but is formed differently and consists of multiple colored rings. Just imagine a round rainbow. It can be seen from an airplane flying above a cloud. The shadow of the airplane appears in the center of the glory—very cool!

The Santa Barbara airport is located just inland from the Pacific Ocean coastline, and often, the fog encroaches upon the airport. Sometimes, after takeoff, you can see a glory on top of the fog layer right below you.

A glory is produced by light backscattered by a combination of reflection, refraction, and diffraction towards its source (the sun) by a cloud of uniformly sized water droplets (fog or cloud). In China, this phenomenon is called Buddha's light. The colorful halo always surrounds the observer's own shadow and in early times, as far back as 63 AD, was thought to show the observer's personal enlightenment.

I don't make that claim, but it is a lovely sight.

Regular rainbows are also nice to see. One day as I was taking off, there was a really large, fully hued bow ahead in my intended flight direction. As I admired it, the tower controller said, "Don't fly through the rainbow and break it."

Pilots never tire of the spectacular scenes we get to witness. Usually it is a solitary savoring, but if there is another flyer in the vicinity sharing the sight, that's nice, too.

I attended a conference on the beauty of flight once. Richard Bach, the author who wrote *Jonathon Livingston Seagull* and several books about flying, was a featured speaker. He recalled one time when he and a friend were each flying a biplane and were treated to a spectacular sunset. One of them picked up his mic and said, "Kinda pretty."—nice understatement.

~~~~~~~~~~~~~

Although Santa Barbara lies next to the Pacific Ocean, the area is very dry. There isn't enough rain most years. One solution to this dilemma is to seed the clouds. Santa Barbara Aviation had a contract to perform this function from an airplane. The plane we used was an elderly Twin Comanche specially fitted with igniters on its wingtips to release silver iodide into the clouds.

Seeding of clouds requires that they contain supercooled liquid water - that is, liquid water colder than zero degrees Celsius. The introduction of a substance such as silver iodide, which has a crystalline structure similar to that of ice, will induce freezing (heterogeneous nucleation).

Cloud-seeding chemicals may be dispersed by aircraft or by dispersion devices located on the ground (generators or canisters fired from anti-aircraft guns or rockets). For release by aircraft, silver iodide flares are ignited and dispersed as an aircraft flies through the inflow of a cloud. This is what we did.

The flight instructors were invited to go along as co-pilots on these flights. While they tended to be bold pilots, they were leery of this gig. Everyone knows you shouldn't deliberately fly at temperatures around 0 degrees Celsius, which is what was effective for this purpose. Nor should you fly when there are rainstorms that might include lightening. So they didn't volunteer.

I did. I was always of the opinion that I shouldn't ask the pilots in my department to do anything I wasn't willing to do.

It was a dark and stormy night—no, really, it was nasty. The Chief Pilot of the charter department and I took off into it.

You can't influence the rainfall unless there is already rain falling, so that's the kind of weather this mission required. After takeoff, we were directed to the military controller at a nearby base, who was in charge of directing our flight. As the hours went on, I reflected that since controllers have trouble steering pilots clear of turbulence, it was amazing how easily he directed us back into it just as we found some smooth air.

It was eerie up there. St. Elmo's fire was a frequent presence on our windscreen—a visible electrical charge that appears blue.

We took turns flying the airplane in the equivalent of holding patterns, at the direction of the controller on the ground. They were easy maneuvers, but it was tiring because of the moderate turbulence, and the St. Elmo's fire didn't encourage us to relax.

At one point, we reported to the ground guy that one of the injectors wasn't functioning. His answer: "Well, can't you fly the plane on one engine?"

That wasn't what we meant, and we definitely wouldn't have kept flying if one of the airplane's engines was shut down. However, we called the company and arranged for a repair on the igniter. That allowed us to land and make a McDonald's run while the repair was made.

The second several hours consisted of more of the same. The rain was falling hard, bringing much-needed moisture to the area, which is really a coastal desert. Any grass you see there has to be irrigated.

At the end of the flight, we decided that one of us would fly the instrument approach, and the other would talk the flying pilot through it. We were that tired.

I did the talking, using the kind of directions I would give an instrument student. "Let's turn to heading 075 to correct. The glideslope is coming in, maintain 120 knots," etc.

It was an interesting experience, and the flight instructors were curious to hear about it. Then they took turns volunteering to fly as co-pilots in the few other cloud seeding flights that year. They were actually disappointed that none of the flights they experienced turned out to be as dicey as the one I've just described.

You can read more about cloud seeding in the online appendix: http://www.awomansplaceisinthecockpit.com/appendix

Chapter 9

Planes, Passengers, and Kids

Cloud seeding wasn't the only flying opportunity that provided a service to the community. For a few years, Santa Barbara Aviation had an advertising deal with KIST, a local AM radio station. Each morning and evening, when it was time for people to be going to work or going home, an SBA pilot would take off in a Beech Sport, fly over the traffic, and make a report on the radio. I seldom did this in the morning because it coincided with the time that I needed to get my kids off to school, but I did a lot of them in the afternoon.

It was a fun gig, flying the plane myself rather than coaching a student. I'd do a quick preflight—the plane was a trainer and had been flying all day, and it had a standing order to be fueled before the scheduled flight. I did always walk around it and check the oil and one fuel tank. Then I'd jump in, start it, and call for taxi clearance.

It seemed that I was often leaving at the last possible minute, and sometimes I'd just tell the controller that I had "the numbers." That implied that I had listened to the Automatic Terminal Information

Service (ATIS) but had forgotten which phonetic alphabetical name that identified the current report.

ATIS is a recording that plays over and over on an aviation communication frequency specific to the particular airport. It includes weather information, which runways are active, and any other significant information about conditions at the airport. It is updated each hour, or more often if there are significant changes. Each time it is modified, it is given a letter designation from the phonetic alphabet.

So when a pilot first contacts a tower before a flight, he/she says, "Santa Barbara Tower, Sport 6602 Romeo at SBA, taxi for takeoff with Alpha." Or Bravo, or Charlie, etc. The name tells the controller that the person has, or hasn't, the current info.

When I said I had the numbers, I was taking responsibility for being aware of the pertinent message. And I would have listened to it within the previous half hour, perhaps on the scanner in the office.

One day, though, when I reported having the numbers, a familiar ground controller came back with, "Oh, you do? What are they?"

Busted! I said, "Oh, sky clear, visibility 10 miles, wind about 240 at 8, altimeter two niner niner two."

"Close enough, taxi to one five right."

What I told him was that the sky was clear with good visibility, which I could see; the wind was blowing from the west-southwest at about eight miles an hour, which I could approximate by looking at the windsock; and the altimeter setting was 29.92 inches of mercury, which I could read from the plane's altimeter. I knew the altimeter in this plane to be pretty accurate, especially at Santa Barbara Airport, which has an altitude of 10 feet above sea level.

Of course, I wouldn't use this shortcut with a student or on a day with bad weather.

Naturally, the controllers all knew me, and they knew about my AirWatch mission. This was in the late seventies, when Santa Barbara

Tower was more relaxed than it became later when the airspace became a terminal radar service area (TRSA) with stricter rules.

As soon as I took off, I'd ask for a frequency change so that I could contact KIST, the radio station. This request would be granted as expeditiously as the ATC person felt it appropriate, considering traffic.

Sport 02Romeo was equipped with a couple of extra radios, so I could talk to the radio station and could also hear their broadcast. Another Sport was the backup plane. It had the radio allowing me to talk to KIST, but not the other one. It served the purpose in a pinch, such as if 02R needed maintenance.

I'd contact the station when the DJ was playing music and was free to talk to me, just to let him know I was in place and ready to make a report. I had only a quick look at the city traffic before my first broadcast, which occurred right before 5 p.m., just prior to the traffic picking up.

Then I'd fly around awhile, over the freeway leading away from the airport toward downtown, checking out the on- and off-ramps and other city streets. Then I went east to Montecito, then back toward the airport, making my second report after the 5 o'clock news.

After my report, I'd have myself positioned at a point that gave me enough time to call the airport tower for clearance to land while proceeding toward the runway.

All of this was pretty simple, except for three things. First, the DJ and the listening public expected me to be funny. Second, if the weather was iffy, it could be more complicated. Third, I usually had a passenger with me.

Being funny wasn't really hard. The late afternoon DJ was a character, and he would feed me ideas or pick up on my quips. I enjoyed the gig and found it easy to banter with him. I'd talk about the quite predictable traffic and then mention something else I could see, such as the ratio of blue to green swimming pools, or the swimming pool inside the Mission grounds.

It was amazing how many people listened to this nonsense. Occasionally, during the time of year when my broadcast would occur as the day turned to night, the DJ would ask everyone listening in cars to flash their lights. I could see them do this, and it was amazing how many of those commuters acknowledged the request.

Sometimes, people I didn't know would approach me in the supermarket or at a party and comment about how they enjoyed the little reports. They would recognize my voice, I guess. A few would complain about my report: "The traffic was heavy yesterday, not moderate."

Santa Barbara traffic just wasn't that variable. The same on-ramps would have a line waiting every day at rush hour. It was rare that an accident impeded the flow.

The second complication, the weather, was trickier. I would fly at 1000 feet, the legal minimum altitude over a populated area. This meant that if the fog rolled in, I was not high enough to be granted an instrument approach. If I could climb before the clouds reached where I was, then I could request and be granted an ILS, or rather a localizer approach, because the plane didn't have glide slope capability.

Usually, the overcast was just high enough that I could safely stay below it and hope that it would stay that way as I jammed back to the airport. If the airport went IFR, meaning that the ceiling was at or below 1000', I'd have to hope that the tower could work me in for a special VFR clearance between the IFR departures and arrivals. The tower guys were sympathetic to my plight and did what they could to help.

Also, there was the United captain who often took off on the long runway just when I was returning, hoping to be worked in on the perpendicular, shorter landing strip that crosses the long one. One day when the weather was closing in fast, he volunteered, "I'll hold for that little airplane." I thanked him as I accepted the magic words, "Air Watch 2, Runway 15, Cleared to land."

This brings us to the third variable: the passenger. KIST and SBA liked to let someone ride along with me. This was fine, as long as the person wasn't scared. One man called me and told me he'd signed up his wife on the passenger waiting list. He said she didn't want to go, but he urged me to talk her into it.

Needless to say, I declined. I was plenty busy on that half-hour flight without having to baby a nervous passenger. I would have been happy to do that on a flight he paid for, when she would have received my full attention. Well, maybe not happy, but willing. But this flight was a freebee and very popular.

If for some reason our waiting list dwindled, all I needed to do was mention on the air that people could call the FBO to be put on the list. This always resulted in a bunch of calls. Sometimes the person manning the front desk in the office would say, "Please don't give out the phone number today; I have a lot of work to do."

There was a bunch of people, many kids (whose parents' written permission was required), who went along as often as we'd let them. Some would have come every day if we hadn't rationed them to no more than once a month. These passengers were easy; they got to know the ropes, when to be quiet, and when they could ask to try flying the plane.

One very nice guy in the military (not as a pilot but a crew member on a helicopter) gave me a surprise. As we were approaching to land, cleared for a straight in approach to Runway 25, with the sun directly in our eyes, we both were annoyed by flicker vertigo. I made some minimizing remark as I added a little power. He was quiet. I looked at him and discovered that he was worried.

I questioned him and found that he thought we were in dire straits. You see, while I could very easily change the RPM of the propeller in the little plane so that the flicker would go away, he was used to a helicopter, which didn't allow for this alteration. Of course, a helicopter doesn't need to land into the sun and can avoid the phenomenon that way, but he knew we had to land straight ahead.

He was so frightened that I asked the tower for a switch to Runway 15. They granted the request, and we turned away. Yes, I had already changed the speed of the prop, eliminating the problem, but he was such a nice guy, and he feared for his life.

~~~~~~~~~~~~~~

I would tell the DJ who my passenger was and some little thing about him or her. For example, I'd say "John is a junior at San Marcos High School" or "Kim is eager to see her house from up here." The DJ would say something to the passenger, hoping to get a reply, but usually would be rewarded with a couple of words or none at all.

One day, the DJ asked, "Why won't they ever talk to me?"

"They have mic fright," I responded.

"Why?"

"They're afraid of sounding foolish."

"Why aren't we afraid of sounding foolish, Beth?"

"Because we already know that we are!"

It was true. If I worried about how my silly remarks might sound, I'd be quiet, too.

People would ask me when I planned what I would say in my reports. The truth was, I didn't even think about it until I was on the flight. Usually, what popped out of my mouth hadn't had any time in my brain before that instant. And, of course, the DJ's tongue was agile. It was fun.

My kids didn't find it amusing. They would complain that their friends talked about my banter, but they found it trite and somewhat embarrassing: "I heard about your latest goofy joke, Mom. It wasn't very funny." What surprised them was that their friends enjoyed my humor.

~~~~~~~~~~~~~

My children were introduced to the airport and flying when they were seven and five. It became commonplace and sometimes boring to them. When we would take a family trip in a plane, they would sit in the back seats and ask when we would get there, not caring that it was much quicker to fly than drive. They just wanted to get there.

The first time we took a trip of two hours or so, they tired of the wads of sugarless gum I always gave children to help their ears adapt to altitude changes. When we returned the Club plane to the home airport, I discovered they had deposited the unwrapped chews into the ashtrays, and they were badly stuck.

I took the trays home, put them in the freezer, easily removed the gum, and returned the trays to the plane the next day. That didn't happen again.

One time when I thought everyone was asleep, I circled around something of interest below us. Soon, a little male voice said, "Mom, does this mean that it will take longer?"

When the children were little and accompanied me to the airport just to hang out, I realized that I could tell them that it was ok to talk to anybody. Of course, this was at an FBO, not at the commercial terminal. It felt good to be able to tell them this—I was usually cautioning them not to answer strange adults.

Not that there were no "strange" people at the airport. There were some real characters, like the line guy who tried to persuade Christa to jump off the FBO roof, reasoning that if she wasn't able to soar, her young bones would at least heal fast.

Later, when I was trying to characterize a most unusual character, a friend of mine, I looked to Christa and asked her to describe John. She thought a moment and then said, "He's an airport person."

~~~~~~~~~~~~~

Being a pilot did allow me to treat my family to some very nice trips. Beautiful Sedona, Arizona, was a favorite of ours for some long weekends. It took less than three hours in the Bonanza.

We also took trips to visit our families in the Midwest. One memorable flight was to visit my parents at their retirement home, where they lived all year except for the winter. It was in northern Minnesota. We were about to fly past Fargo, ND, when I called the tower to tell them that we were just transiting the area enroute to Dell Rapids. The controller told me that there was tornado activity ahead, so I asked for a landing on any runway. I was cleared immediately, and we taxied to a local FBO.

We were greeted by a fuel truck, driven by a young man who inquired if I would like the plane to be hangared for the night. I said no.

Another man joined us, and again we were asked if we wanted to be towed to a hangar. I didn't usually do that, but I asked what the fee was. When I was told that it was five dollars a night, I agreed.

My husband and daughter went with the airplane to help unload it; my son stayed with me. And then a roar announced a big gust of wind, not a tornado but pretty fierce. I pulled my little boy behind me to shield him. After the gust abated, I found that my hair was full of tiny pebbles, and my skin felt a bit prickly. It was a good thing I had gotten the plane into a hangar.

We walked to the FBO office to arrange payment for the night and refueling. While there, I called my dad and asked him to pick us up—a forty-mile drive.

Once I had that arranged, I called the control tower to ask if we could come up for a visit. It was hot, and we needed to wait for an hour or so. I thought my family would enjoy seeing it, too.

There wasn't much to see. The controllers said they had called their families and told them to seek shelter. Flights were being diverted because of the weather.

Then we saw it: a tornado in the distance! I had a camera and took a few pictures of it. And then it was over. We enjoyed a nice visit with my parents at their home on a little lake.

~~~~~~~~~~~~~~

That wasn't the only trip where the weather changed our plans. Another time, I had flown my family to Sedona, AZ, for a Beech Aero Club fly-in. There were several planeloads of people along on the trip. I waited until everyone else was safely in the air before taking off. Unfortunately, that put us into the turbulence that often accompanies hot early autumn afternoons.

After awhile, the kids got sick. They were sufficiently uncomfortable that I landed at the closest airport with facilities. All we needed was somewhere air-conditioned to hang out. Twentynine Palms fit the bill.

We found the local flight school and fuel facility. As is usual at small airports, the people were friendly. When it hadn't cooled down by the time the owner wanted to go home (it was Father's Day and his son had planned a nice dinner for five o'clock or so), he simply asked us to lock the door when we left. I wasn't surprised; I've done the same thing.

We waited until dark, which brought cooler air and calmer skies. Then we locked the door and taxied for takeoff.

I began the run-up, switched from both magnetos to the right, and got no drop in rpm. Although I was pretty sure what would happen, I went to the left mag and, sure enough, there was silence. So there I was, contemplating a night flight with just one magneto.

There are two so that if one fails, there is the redundancy of another. If I had been by myself or if it was daytime, I would have gone. The chances are slight that the other mag would fail in flight. But I didn't go.

So we returned to the only spot available on the field: the little FBO I had just locked. At least it wasn't hot anymore.

There was a telephone booth, and I called SBA, the company where I worked in Santa Barbara. An on-call charter pilot was located, and he picked us up in a Baron because he didn't want to fly a single-engine plane at night—redundancy again. It was expensive, but I didn't argue.

~~~~~~~~~~~~~~

Another time, we took a family trip to Death Valley. California pilots like to fly into Death Valley at least once, because the runway is below sea level. It looks odd on the altimeter.

Of course, you want to choose your day. It is cold in the winter and extremely hot in summer. Avoid the summer.

I flew my family there in May of 1978 for a Beech Aero Club overnight fly-in. Several planeloads of club members and passengers went on the trip. We enjoyed the altitude phenomenon, saw the sights, had dinner and socialized, and flew back the next day.

During the day, my nine-year-old daughter wandered off. I couldn't see her anywhere. She was old enough that she wouldn't panic, but I was worried that she might be scared. There were lots of tourists milling about, but I chose an unlikely group to ask for help: a big gaggle of Hells Angels.

An unlikely option? Maybe so, but they were willing, spread the word, and soon located her. I'd described her as a nine-year-old copy of me, dressed in a light blue t-shirt and blue and white striped pants, so they recognized this lone child.

~~~~~~~~~~~~~~

My kids were often bored at the airport when they were young, and when we went on vacation, they were just as bored during flights as most kids are during car rides. One day when they were little, we attended an air show at Point Mugu. There were some fabulous acts. During one of these, Greg decided that he must visit the Porta Potty right then—no respect for superior aerobatics.

Greg and Christa accompanied me to overnight fly-ins a couple of times when they were very young teens. One time, we went to Porterville, CA. After they tired of the airport scene, they decided to walk into town. When they returned, they reported that there was "nothing to do" in town either.

One time after Christa had washed a school plane at our flight school, she came into the office to tell me that the faucet she'd used was dripping. John Mullane asked her if she planned to dry the plane. When she shook her head, he invited her to go with him and air-dry it.

Realizing that he meant that they would be flying it, which she had never done before, she agreed. But she persisted, "Mom, the faucet won't stop dripping."

John dragged her away to the plane. While they preflighted 24504, Christa asked John to be sure to pay attention in case she did something wrong—she who had never flown before.

John, a very experienced pilot and instructor, talked her through the entire flight, just once around the pattern. Occasionally, she would admonish him to pay attention. A seasoned instructor touches the controls seldom; recovery is always an option and happens fast if needed.

When they landed, I went out to meet them. I asked how the flight went.

"Fine," said Christa.

"What did you do?"

"I took off and landed. But Mom, we need to fix that faucet."

She was definitely not enthusiastic pilot material.

Another time that Christa washed an airplane, she was maybe 16 years old, and she decided to wear a bikini. It was an unusually warm day, and she thought she might as well work on her tan. The young men who fueled airplanes drove by a few times, and they reported that the control tower appeared to be leaning in her direction. When I found this out, I added a sweatshirt to her ensemble.

~~~~~~~~~~~~

One Saturday morning, several planeloads of pilots and families affiliated with our school flew up to Lake Isabella near Bakersfield. Roger, a flight instructor who was about 21 years old, flew our school Cessna 172. He insisted that Greg, then about 17, should sit in the front with access to the controls. Although I had warned him that this was unlikely, Roger was sure that he could spur the interest of Greg. Poor Roger—Greg, not a morning person, slept the whole way.

It turned into a very fun weekend. We landed at Kern County Airport, met the family who ran the FBO, admired the little girl's new baby kitties, were loaned a car to buy groceries, and then walked to the airport campground, where we put up tents.

We swam, sunbathed, and ate—very relaxing. The kids, Roger, Greg, and Christa were determined to catch some fish to add to our camp stove dinner. They were only able to capture one very small specimen. Nevertheless, they breaded it in corn chip fragments and cooked it.

Christa occupied the right front seat on the way home; she stayed awake.

Both kids knew that there was the possibility of them learning to fly, and more importantly, that someone other than their mother would teach them. It was never discussed, and they showed no interest.

That is, they showed no interest until the day I drove Christa north for her first year of college. We saw a beautiful biplane performing a neat acrobatic move and my daughter enthused, "That is so cool!"

I tried to bite my tongue but was unsuccessful and muttered, "Good timing, Christa."

She had really only admired a pretty maneuver; this didn't mean that she suddenly felt a passion for flying. In fact, one day later that year when she, Greg, and I spent the day together in San Francisco, it was pointed out emphatically that I was the only one with aviation addiction.

Both children had been born in San Francisco, and they enjoyed our frequent trips back to see relatives and friends, as well as revisit favorite places. So on this jaunt, I told them that they could decide what to do. Consequently, we rode a cable car.

Just as the conveyance topped a hill, its cable malfunctioned, and we were told that we wouldn't be moving soon. Everyone disembarked and stood admiring the clear view of the bay on a fog-free day. And then the Blue Angels appeared!

I hadn't known that the Angels participate in Fleet Week in the Bay Area every year, doing a show right over the bay, north of the city.

What did the kids say? "Mom, you said we could do what WE wanted to do!"

I don't think they really thought I had arranged the sequence of events.

~~~~~~~~~~~~~

It was after Greg graduated from college that he decided that he would invest in an airplane and lease it back to our school. He did that; N212MB was a nicely equipped Cessna 152. People don't tend to make money from leaseback planes, but when your mom owns the school and helps you find a plane that will be popular, the odds improve quite a bit. It worked out well; he made some money, and the extra radios made the plane not only a good IFR trainer but a favorite for cross-country rentals, as well.

With no pressure or even a suggestion from me, Greg decided that as an airplane owner, he should try taking flying lessons. He liked his instructor, did his homework, and became a private pilot. I didn't fly with him at all until he had earned his private pilot certificate. I had other people do his stage checks, and his checkride was with an FAA inspector—not easy, but not his mother!

The first time we flew together, we went to a fly-in, checked out the antique airplanes, and spent the night with some of our friends, all of us in sleeping bags under the wings of our planes. When we arrived back in Santa Barbara, people asked Greg what it was like flying with me. He said it was fine except that I told him to look outside more. That produced a few chuckles; most everyone at our school had heard that direction from me.

Friends and relatives enjoyed little scenic flights with Greg, and he liked introducing them to N212MB, his Cessna 152.

Eventually, Greg acquired a bunch of certificates and ratings and worked as an instructor at our flight school. We enjoyed working together. Eventually, after a few years, he took over some of my responsibilities and became Chief Flight Instructor of most of the courses. Now he is an airline captain.

Chapter 10

Challenging Airplanes

The disadvantage of not being an airline pilot is that you don't get to fly any big jets. I was fortunate in having opportunities to fly some really nice small jets and the occasional turboprop a little here and there. Here's an example.

One day that I had scheduled myself for non-urgent chief flight instructor paperwork, I noticed a little consternation emanating from a friend of mine, who was talking to a man in a suit. I eavesdropped a bit and learned that Jim was about to take his Citation jet type rating checkride with the suit. Jim had a client with a Citation, so he needed to be checked out in this type of aircraft. The problem seemed to be that the check airman did not want to accept a handwritten application form, and Jim didn't know how to type.

I walked across the lobby and offered to do the job. I'm a fast typist and like to do a favor for a friend. It was no big deal, but my unexpected reward was really great. Jim and the suit asked if I'd like to go along on the flight. Of course! I never turned down the opportunity to have a ride in a super nice high-performance plane.

The checkride was interesting, but what came next was outstanding. The designated examiner terminated the test at his home airport in Orange County. Jim was tired and asked if I would like to fly back to Santa Barbara. The other Citation rated pilot onboard was a friend. I'd checked him out in a little plane a few years before. He agreed that I could fly; obviously he would be pilot-in-command.

What fun that was! Of course, it doesn't take long to get from John Wayne Airport to Santa Barbara in a quick business jet, but I savored every minute.

When I called for taxi clearance out of the departure airport, the controller gave me instructions and then asked if I had chosen the plane's paint scheme. I recall inexactly that it was blue and orange, rather unusual. I suppose this ATC guy thought it must have been designed by a woman. Actually, I have no idea who chose the colors; it certainly wasn't me.

The airplane was easy to fly. It handled like a big Cessna, which it was. The flight was uneventful except that when we got back to SBA, I was issued a go-around order because of traffic ahead of us not clearing the runway in time. We were just a couple hundred feet from touching down. I had heard that jets take awhile to spool up for last-minute aborted landings, so I was a tad nervous for a second or two, but it worked fine—just like any Cessna—and I got to fly the pattern, adding a few minutes to my adventure.

~~~~~~~~~~~~

"In a twin-engine aircraft, the purpose of the second engine is to supply the pilot with enough power to fly to the scene of the crash."

Acquiring a multiengine rating has two distinct sections. The first is like checking out in any airplane—getting to know the systems and flying all the usual maneuvers. The second is a whole different experience. It is all about what happens when one of the engines quits, and what to do about it.

All the possible scenarios are demonstrated and practiced, most of them at about 5000 feet above the ground so there is plenty of room to recover when mistakes are made. My multiengine instructor made a point of having me perform a couple of these maneuvers, including a Vmc demonstration at about 1000 feet AGL. That really got my attention and showed how dangerous it would be if an engine really quit at that altitude or below and the correct measures were not swiftly taken. (I was already a flight instructor at this point.)

Vmc is the minimum controllable airspeed of a multiengine aircraft that is operating on a single engine. It is determined by worst conditions: maximum gross weight, center of gravity location, critical engine loss simulated, etc. When one of the engines is lost, the airplane reacts by turning in the direction of the dead engine. Because of the loss of power from the second engine, the airplane loses airspeed. If pilot doesn't compensate for the turn with the rudder and reduce pressure on the yoke, the plane can reach a speed that is below the single engine minimum controllable airspeed. And then it can't go straight.

It's odd; people get used to the idea that if they lose power in a single-engine plane, they must immediately lower the nose to maintain the attitude that will give them the most efficient glide while preparing to do an emergency landing. However, with a twin, the multiengine rated pilot who doesn't fly often and seldom practices emergency procedures is likely to fail to change the attitude. It is counterintuitive to think that an airplane can't necessarily hold its altitude while at least one engine is operating.

I attended a CFI refresher clinic during which a speaker asked the instructors what rating they enjoyed teaching the most. I was one of the minority who didn't favor the multiengine rating. Granted, the folks who attend these clinics are almost exclusively part-time instructors who support themselves with a full-time non-flying job. For them, the multi students probably provide their only chance to fly twins. Or maybe they just enjoy danger.

Students learning to fly multiengine airplanes are the most lethal. Not only do they do things that they know they are not supposed to do, they may even have just announced the correct procedure before forsaking it.

For example, I had one student who was nice guy and a good student, using the GI bill to pay 90% of his fees. He was working on the rating full time; wasn't married, so he could spend as much time as he wanted. He loved flying and did his homework. I've called him IMS for ideal multi student.

When both engines are functioning, flying a twin is just like flying any other complex airplane. We achieved this first part of the multiengine rating just fine.

Then came the second phase, which is when engines are failed by the instructor and the student rectifies the situation. Most of the work is done at altitude, where there is plenty of air below in which to recover. However, an early lesson includes simulating an engine failure on the runway while taking off.

IMS had read all about it. He told me the procedure in our ground session prior to flight. We taxied to the runway, hold short, and I asked him to tell me again what we are about to do. He correctly replied, "I pull back both throttles and brake the airplane to a stop."

Correct. This sequence, along with correct rudder usage, keeps the plane going straight down the runway.

Then I told him that I would pull the left engine. What would he do?

He once again answered positively, "I will bring back both throttles and bring the plane to a stop."

I told him that I would handle the radio so that he could think only of the maneuver. After we received clearance from the tower, he taxied onto Runway 15R and added power to both engines. Shortly thereafter, I reached up and retarded the left engine. What did IMS do? Did he pull back both throttles?

No. He decided to continue the takeoff roll and maintained full power on the right engine. So the airplane was at liftoff speed, and even though I moved quickly, it was off the ground before I could add power to the idle engine. This slight delay allowed the plane to begin a turn, so we took off aiming toward the side of the runway. We barely missed the runway lights. Oh, yes, we were departing from Runway 15R, the lighted one. Also, because it was the right parallel, we were moving towards 15L.

Obviously, I was flying the plane at that point. Having added full power to the left engine, I got us steered back to the correct path. Meanwhile, my student was completely stunned.

He had no words to explain. He didn't know why he did it. He was sorry he nearly killed us or wrecked the plane. He couldn't even talk at the time.

I told the tower that we wanted to go around the pattern to land, and after I touched down and taxied back, I thought that the oddest thing about all of this was that the tower made no mention of the fact that we appeared to have taken off on a non-existent Runway 18.

Poor IMS was completely drained, and after I talked to him a few minutes, I sent him home to recover. In the next couple of weeks, we completed the rating and there were no further surprises. But that's why I don't put multiengine ratings near the top of my favorite things to teach.

I never felt that my job as an instructor was complete until a person learned firsthand that he/she could make that mistake. Until they experience it, most people don't believe it could happen.

Up at several thousand feet, there is plenty of time to recover if the pilot reduces the power on the operating engine rather than the dead one. If it were to happen while approaching to land or just after takeoff, it could be bad.

Bad results don't tend to happen because of just one thing; more likely, several individual things went wrong. It seems simple enough to remember and act on "dead foot, dead engine," which means that when a rudder pedal doesn't respond, that indicates engine failure on the same side of the plane. Hopefully, anyone with a multiengine rating will respond correctly. But if it occurs while something else is occurring—for example, communication with ATC, a passenger with a need, or poor weather—this increases the likelihood of an incorrect reaction.

Pilots who fly twins every day and practice emergency procedures on a regular basis don't tend to make those errors. It's the person who takes lightly the responsibility to stay very current that is susceptible. A good multiengine pilot always rehearses in his/her mind what is to be done if an engine fails during the takeoff roll, after liftoff with usable runway underneath, and after there is no available runway.

~~~~~~~~~~~~~

You know you've landed with the wheels up when it takes full power to taxi to the ramp.

Another thing many pilots are certain will never happen to them is landing with the gear retracted. Young pilots are especially prone to be certain they will never make this mistake. Therefore, I always created a situation where they nearly landed with the wheels up.

When pilots transition to complex airplanes, there are more things that can go wrong. A significantly more complicated airplane can fatigue the pilot who is getting familiar with it. There are new systems to understand and new procedures to handle.

I would deliberately have a long lesson in which we worked through a lot of new things, and then I would distract the student as we were entering the traffic pattern. I'd handle the communications and tell the tower that we would be simulating a gear up approach. I'd ask that the controller not repeat my request.

Meanwhile, because of the distraction, the pilot didn't extend the landing gear. Nor did he hear that our landing clearance was for "the option," which meant we could land or not. What he/she was struggling with was the fact that the airplane wasn't descending as well as expected from previous approaches. Which, of course, was due to the lack of drag caused by the gear still being in the wheel wells.

The student would add full flaps and take off all the power, and still the airplane was too high. Sometimes he/she would even do the GUMP check—gas, undercarriage, mixture, prop—but wouldn't notice that the undercarriage was still up. The habit, newly ingrained, was just an oral reassurance that all had been done, without actually checking to see that each step had indeed been accomplished.

I know this sounds unlikely, but this was a tired pilot, doing new tricks at 90 mph or more. Not a lot of time passed. Finally, close to the runway, I pointed out that the gear was not down. Often, my poor student would freeze, and I would initiate the go-around and maybe even do the entire approach and landing. We would have an interesting postflight debriefing that day.

It's commonly said that as far as gear-up landings go, there are those who have done one and those that will. That is why I played this nasty trick on my students. Hopefully, it would never happen to them through their own fault.

I never landed with the gear up, but I did have a few scares. SBA's simplest complex trainer, Sierra 3 Papa Tango, had a tendency to occasionally sound its gear warning horn when the gear was in fact extended. I would go through all the checks, verify that the plane "felt" like it was down, call the company, get the maintenance chief on the radio. Sometimes I'd even do a flyby of the tower, where the controller would announce that the gear appeared to be down. It was nerve-wracking to land, for fear that it wasn't locked.

One time, I was doing a test flight on 3PT after it had extensive maintenance. The mechanic who had done most of the work asked to go along. I let him fly the plane; he wasn't a pilot, but all mechanics know how to work the controls. They have to taxi planes quite often.

At altitude, we were cycling the gear as Mike, the head of maintenance, had requested. Nothing felt right. The airplane made weird noises. Mike was in the office, listening to the radio, when I called and said I was returning and why. Mike and John, the chief pilot, decided that they would get into another plane and come up and take a look.

So they did. We met up in the practice area. John maneuvered the Sundowner below us, and 3PT looked good to them.

We all returned for landing; they went first. Normally, I would let the mechanic land the plane with my coaching, but I took over when we were on base leg and landed the plane very slowly, very lightly.

When we were off the runway, taxiing back, I asked ground control to have the Sundowner go to company frequency (both airplanes had two communications radios). Then I let them listen to the gear horn, which was howling. I taxied carefully to the shop. When Mike put the plane up on a lift and cycled the gear in the air, it didn't work. Oh boy, that was a close one!

~~~~~~~~~~~~

Sometimes pilots have to land with at least one landing gear retracted, because of a malfunction. I always feel sorry for those guys; it isn't their fault, but they feel bad anyway. If it is just one of the three wheels, they try as hard as they can to let that part of the plane settle gently, but it doesn't feel good to hear a plane scrape the pavement. They even land on a portion of the runway that will cause as little inconvenience as possible to subsequent traffic while the plane is being moved. You don't taxi with a wheel up!

There was one pilot who had a Mitsubishi, a turboprop twin, who really shut the airport down. He forgot to put the gear down, and his plane came to rest at the intersection of runways 25 and 15R. That meant that one runway wasn't affected—15L—but unfortunately, it happened as the sky was getting dark. 15L wasn't usable at night because it was not lighted.

Chapter 11

Challenging Airports

A irports all have at least one runway, of course, but those runways can be quite different due to a variety of factors. One of the more difficult concepts to get across to students is the effect of high density altitude, which is the altitude that a normally aspirated airplane engine "thinks" it is experiencing on hot days. It is more serious when the hot day occurs at an airport that's physically 5000-7000 feet above sea level, because the airplane will react as if it were about 2000 feet higher than that.

We would simulate this condition by limiting the amount of power that the student could use for takeoff, and while that gives a very realistic demonstration, it doesn't convince the student. He or she knows that the only reason that the plane didn't perform strongly was that I was controlling the throttle and that there was more power available.

It is important that pilots understand high density altitude because, if they don't, they may find themselves unable to take off from a high, hot runway someday. I remember the first time I encountered this. I was departing from Big Bear, which has an altitude of 6750 feet. I nearly aborted the takeoff because the Cessna 182 I was flying felt like a 172. I knew that would happen after I calculated the density altitude and the length of runway that would be required. I knew I had sufficient length, but still, it was daunting to experience the phenomenon. I'll never forget it, and I strongly recommended that students who planned to travel to high airports experience the effect before taking a load of their friends on a flight like that.

~~~~~~~~~~~~~

Another situation that really needs to be experienced to be believed is the effect of runway gradient. My students and I encountered this challenge at the airport at Santa Catalina Island.

When I first flew to The Airport in the Sky as a private pilot, I was a bit nervous about the arrival because Runway 22 was considered tricky. Not only does the runway slope, it's placed atop a flat portion of the island with each end occupying an edge of the available land. The approach end begins at the edge of a 1500-foot cliff. This gives the airport some characteristics similar to landing on an aircraft carrier that is 1,602 feet in the air. There aren't any familiar visual cues for altitude reference—I had to rely on the altimeter. In addition, there is often a strong downdraft caused by the prevailing winds falling over the cliff. This often meant that extra power needed to be added on short final.

So, of course, the inexperienced pilot will decide to land long, which isn't a good idea because the runway isn't very lengthy. The fact that it isn't flat only makes things worse. The first 2000 feet slants uphill, and the remainder is flat. Because of this, the strip appears even shorter than it is.

An uphill slant causes mistakes in landings. It appears as if you are too high on approach, and unless you realize that this is an illusion, you may actually come in too low, requiring even more power and probably an awkward arrival.

You can simulate the look of a flat runway by holding your arm straight out from your shoulder, palm down and your hand flat. This is what a level runway looks like on a normal 3 - 5 degree approach. Now, tilt your hand up 10 degrees. This is the view you see when approaching an upslope runway. The illusion tells you that you're too high. The potential danger is that you will respond to the illusion rather than the reality and come in too low.

When it was time to leave, the uphill slope of Runway 22 again caused concern. The runway looked very short and also, because of the gradient, aircraft on the opposite end of the runway aren't visible. Furthermore, the uphill slant increases the distance covered on the takeoff roll. So I crossed my fingers that nobody was departing in the opposite direction and that the airport advisory frequency was manned by someone who was paying attention.

In case you are curious, the gradient or slope of the runway is the amount of change in runway height over the length of the runway. The gradient is expressed as a percentage, such as a 3% gradient. This means that for every 100 feet of runway length, the runway height changes by 3 feet. A positive gradient indicates that the runway height increases, and a negative gradient indicates that the runway decreases in height. An up-sloping runway impedes acceleration and results in a longer ground run during takeoff. However, landing on an up-sloping runway typically reduces the landing roll. A down-sloping runway aids in acceleration on takeoff, resulting in shorter takeoff distances. The opposite is true when landing, as landing on a down-sloping runway increases landing distances.

The next time I was preflighting for a flight to Catalina, several people pointed out that it was a dangerous airport, and my passengers overheard them. Kay was not fond of flying, as I had learned when I took her flying in Washington State. Hearing these remarks didn't increase her enthusiasm for the trip. I explained about how the runway had gotten its reputation, and she climbed aboard.

It was a gorgeous day, and there were whales cavorting in the ocean. My group of three passengers all thoroughly enjoyed the sights, so it was a fun flight. Even the approach to Runway 22 was easy because a visual slope indicator had been installed. All a pilot needed to do was follow its 3-degree glide path to maintain the correct approach path.

Actually, the only heart-pounding part of the day came with the 25-minute trip to and from the town of Avalon. The van drivers zoom around the many curves. Fortunately, there is little or no traffic—there are few vehicles on the island.

It's fun to spend a few hours or more in Avalon. During the summer, it is overrun with tourists; a visit before Memorial Day or after Labor Day is preferable. You can hang out on the beach, rent a variety of water vehicles, or go on various types of boating tours. You can snorkel or scuba or go rafting or fishing. My favorite is viewing the rampant marine life through the floor of a glass-bottom boat.

Of course, there are a lot of beach towns in California that provide opportunities for fun. But you could drive to those.

~~~~~~~~~~~~

Despite the challenging runway, Santa Catalina Island is an appealing destination from Santa Barbara. It's a beautiful flight over the ocean, and sometimes you can see the whales jumping. I don't recommend low ocean flying in a single-engine plane because of the scarcity of emergency landing sites. However, it only requires about 9,000 or 10,000 feet of altitude to always be within range of land if the route is planned carefully. So it's doable in a small plane.

When I was working as a flight instructor for the Beech Aero Club, members of the club flew to Catalina twice. The first trip was pleasantly uneventful. I was in the right seat of a four-place Sundowner owned by student pilot Bob. His two children were in back. As we neared the island, Bob stared at the aircraft carrier-like formation of the runway, sitting 1600 feet in the air. He pretty much stopped thinking and acting. I began talking to him and gently nudged the little plane into the attitude he was neglecting to effect. His son, a young teenager, correctly read the situation and began taunting Dad.

He had already inquired why I was along. I'd replied that Dad could not take passengers yet and needed an instructor along to make the flight legal. I explained that the airport was a bit challenging and I might need to help a little. "A little!" this sweet child guffawed.

Son was ready to embarrass Dad when the opportunity arose—these were not tightly disciplined children. So I told the boy to be quiet until we were on the ground. It's funny how kids recognize a tone of unarguable authority.

Bob was not one to spend a great deal of time planning a trip. He could get by with this when he was supported by an instructor, although he had to learn to do all the steps before he received his private pilot certificate. As a result of little or no prior study of the destination airport, he pretty much sat in shock as I maneuvered the aircraft around the pattern to a landing.

And then everyone had a relaxing day at the beach.

The second trip was planned and anticipated by several private pilots plus two planeloads of students with an instructor in each of them. Unfortunately, the weather at Santa Catalina that morning was persistently IFR. That was a big disappointment for most of the intended adventurers, who hoped until the last minute that the conditions would improve.

Most flights were cancelled; just two planes went. The other instructor (Rick) and I each went in the right seat of a Bonanza, letting the amateur pilots fly most of the way but taking over nearing the island.

Most often, we can talk people through the instrument approach, but this one was tricky. Of course, there was no radar facility on the island. We were communicating with Los Angeles Center, and in this situation, only one plane at a time is cleared for the approach. I requested the clearance first, so Rick had to circle while I maneuvered through the clouds. He was the lucky one; I nearly had a heart attack!

I kept the speed up so that Rick wouldn't have to wait long. I slowed as I neared the airport and broke out of the clouds approaching Runway 4, as directed. On short final, I heard that the airport has just been declared VFR. As a result, I saw that a plane was taking off on the opposite end, headed toward me. Of course, I missed the approach and circled to land at the other end.

I don't like heart-pounding landings! I vowed never to fly to the Airport in the Sky again on a day when instrument and visual flight rule procedures might collide.

~~~~~~~~~~~~~~

Other airports also have issues with runway gradient. My beautiful little red Citabria was crashed by a pilot who flew it to Taft without learning about the effects of slope on the approach to a sloping landing strip. When approaching a downsloping runway, it appears foreshortened; this gives the illusion that you are low. On the other hand, an upsloping strip looks stretched and provides the illusion that the approach is too high. A pilot needs to recognize that this will happen and not allow him- or herself to go by the visual effect. Otherwise, the runway will be overshot or undershot.

An unusually wide or narrow runway provides another illusion. Early in my flying career, I was taking off on a particularly wide runway and was assigned an intersection from which to depart. I taxied onto the runway, but as I was aligning the plane, I noticed that the runway looked really short. I asked the tower controller what the remaining length was and learned that it was over 3000 feet—plenty of room. It just looked short because of the width.

Later, after I had become the Chief Flight Instructor for Santa Barbara Aviation, I flew the general manager to LAX. He had been a military pilot but hadn't flown in years. When it was time to depart for our return flight, there was a long line of planes waiting for their turns. There often was at Los Angeles International Airport, but it was worse than usual that day because of construction on Runway 25L, one of the four LAX runways.

I had taken a peek at the disabled runway during my approach to landing. So I had an idea: I asked Ground Control if I could have an intersection takeoff on the last quarter of 24L. He agreed, knowing that I was flying a small airplane, probably a Bonanza. I got almost immediate takeoff clearance because the airlines couldn't operate on that short a takeoff surface. As I taxied into position, the GM got a tad nervous and asked how much runway we had. I assured him that we had 2500 feet, plenty for our plane at sea level.

~~~~~~~~~~~~~~

Of course, gradient and other optical illusions aren't the only things that can make a runway challenging. The Channel Islands, which lie off the southern coast of Santa Barbara, boast a few challenging runways. (Yes, there is a southern coastline; unlike much of California, the Santa Barbara area is bounded by a range of mountains to the north that run east and west, and the Pacific Ocean to the south, parallel to the mountains.)

A few of the islands have landing strips. Generally, they are not available to pilots, but when I worked for Santa Barbara Aviation, the company had contracts to provide charter services to two of them. Therefore, I had the opportunity to land on them occasionally. The runway on Santa Rosa was challenging in several ways. First, it was bumpy. Add to that the fact that it wasn't entirely straight. And then, because of the location, it was prone to updrafts and downdrafts most days. I found myself encountering a nasty downdraft on short approach and had to add full power to make a decent landing. Some days it was easier to take off from the grass right next to the runway, and I tended to do that.

And then there was San Miguel Island's strip. I only went there once. The island was owned by the US military, and I can't remember the reason for the flight, but I do remember the approach. I knew about where the runway was, but you really couldn't see it very well because it was an unmarked grass strip. You knew you were in the right place on short final as you saw the No Trespassing signs on either side.

The day I landed there, the grass was quite long. On my next flight, which was to LAX in the same plane, the tower asked me to turn on my landing light, which was already on. I wondered if they were having trouble seeing it because it was green—grassy green.

~~~~~~~~~~~~~

The tightest field I ever negotiated when flying for pleasure was the Missouri Valley, Iowa, landing strip. I flew my family in my Bonanza into this small town for my parents' fiftieth wedding anniversary in 1977. My older brother David and his family lived there, and they hosted the party.

I mistakenly looked no farther than the field length printed on the Omaha sectional chart. Had I checked the Airport Facility Directory, I would have learned that the strip was shorter than the 2000' I had read on the sectional, and I would have planned to land in nearby Omaha.

My first clue that the airport was iffy came from the Center controller with whom I was communicating. When I cancelled my IFR clearance upon reaching better weather, I asked for a frequency change. The friendly controller suggested that I stay with him until I had spotted Missouri Valley. That got my attention, and I remained on his screen.

As I neared the airport, the ATC guy asked if I had it in sight. When I replied in the affirmative, he asked if I still planned to land there. I did. He wished me a friendly good day, and I changed frequencies to alert the local traffic (of which there was none) of my intent to land at Missouri Valley.

The field was short and had grass growing on it, but it accommodated our arrival just fine. It would also be long enough for our takeoff in a couple of days, if I didn't refuel. We had enough fuel for about an hour and a half flight and didn't need that much.

Two days later, after my parents headed for home in their car, we said goodbye to Dave's family and he drove us to the airport. Conditions had worsened. There was light rain and a lowering overcast. The clouds posed no problem; I filed an IFR clearance to Omaha, which I would pick up once I was airborne. Rain on a grass runway, however, decreases the performance of the airplane.

Luckily, I was flying an excellent plane and was on the top of my game. Using a combination of soft and short field techniques, I lifted off as soon as ground effect would support us along with our small amount of fuel, accelerated to best angle of climb and then to best rate of climb, and called Center to get my clearance before we entered the clouds.

I immediately received an IFR approach clearance for ILS 14R to Omaha's Eppley Airfield. Within 20 minutes, I was on the ground again, this time on a state-of-the-art instrument runway.

~~~~~~~~~~~~~

Of course, an airport like LAX or SFO is the opposite type of challenge: very busy, lots of big jets, very few little planes. It took me a while to be brave enough to land at San Francisco, even though my family flew with me up to the city fairly often. Once I had the Bonanza, though, it really worked well. That plane could approach at the same speeds as the airlines.

Once I was proficient in it, I really got a kick out of keeping up with the jets. At the time, Butler Aviation was very friendly to us little guys, and all the services and IFR procedures made it a much more welcoming option than Half Moon Bay.

Complicated airport layouts are easy to figure out from the sky, but on the ground, not so much. One time, I was assigned a small, seldom-used runway, and I just couldn't figure out where it was. Fortunately, radar controlled fields have a service called progressive taxi instructions. The ground controller tells you when and where to turn. I think I heard him chuckle when he agreed to guide me.

~~~~~~~~~~~~

If you have ever been near LAX on a clear night, you are likely to see a long string of airplanes from east to west for many miles, all in line for landing at the airport, which has four parallel runways. *How would an airplane get into that huge lineup without going about 100 miles to the east to get a place?* I wondered the first time I flew to LAX from Santa Barbara.

I learned that there is a solution. I could fly south just off the coastline and then, as I neared the airport, I would be given a sequence, which means that a controller would tell me which airplane I could follow. I had to report the plane in sight, and when I did, I would be issued a clearance to land, and I could maneuver to stay sufficiently behind the airliner so that I wouldn't be in anyone's way. An airplane like a Bonanza can easily manage that; slower types aren't easily worked into the system.

~~~~~~~~~~~~

Runways need to be long enough to accommodate the airplanes that will use them. Also, they take a lot of punishment each time a heavy airplane encounters them. Both of these things require runways to be shut down for maintenance or reconstruction now and then. This happened in Santa Barbara occasionally without huge impact, but one year the longest runway, 7/25, needed a month-long redo.

The two other runways remained open, except for very brief periods when the areas of them that intersected 7/25 were being worked on, one at a time. Although large airliners could not operate on Santa Barbara airport for the entire period that the long runway was shut down, most planes could. On sunny days, there was little impact for them. Fortunately, the work was done during a time of year when the weather was generally good.

However, there were days when instrument approaches were necessary in order to land. For this reason, a taxiway parallel to 7/25 was temporarily promoted to runway status. It was the one on which the heaviest airplanes normally taxied, so it could handle a lot of weight. The precision IFR approach—ILS 7—could then be used, although the minimum altitude that one could descend to without seeing the runway was higher than the usual 200 feet AGL. That's because, after breaking out of the clouds or fog, we had to sidestep from the localizer course (which led to 7) and land on 7R.

The day the temporary runway was open, I was taxiing for takeoff, headed for 15, when I decided that I wanted to be the first person to use the temporary runway. I called Ground Control and asked if I could go to 25L instead. I was granted that taxi clearance and then, after we performed our run-up, I asked for takeoff clearance. I heard, "Sport 6602R, Santa Barbara Tower, cleared for takeoff Runway 25L." It was a little thing, but still, I was the first.

The construction was completed right on schedule. There are large financial penalties to be paid if the contractors don't complete on time. A delay would have cost the airlines, the airport, and thus the city of Santa Barbara a lot of money in lost revenue—not to mention the inconvenience to passengers who lost their convenient flights on United.

Flight students, too, sometimes had to pay for extra taxi time when 7/25 couldn't be crossed. Everyone was relieved when 7/25 was back in service, complete with its updates and smooth new surface.

Chapter 12

People and Planes

W hen I started working at SBA, Pete McGowan was the head of the flight school. He was a crusty old guy, indeed. He had been flying long hours for many, many years. It was quite a surprise when he announced that he was retiring from SBA. His plan was to move north and run a worm farm—kind of like running a flight school.

An FAA-Approved Flight School cannot be without a chief flight instructor for very long. That's probably why Pete's successor was hired; it needed to be quick.

To think that Pete seemed difficult to work with! This guy, whom I will call Henry, was not only difficult but very odd. He and his wife both loved to boast about his wonderful career, both in the military and as a civilian. His flying was strange, though.

One day, he wanted to go along with me on the AirWatch. So, of course, I agreed and he occupied the right seat of Sport 02R. He wanted to fly while I was doing the first traffic report, and of course, that was fine. What wasn't fine was that he decided to fly it slow, "to save on fuel."

I didn't care about that; what I didn't like was that he flew so slowly that the stall warning came on and buzzed loudly. When he didn't correct for that, I shoved the nose down, added power, and took over the airplane. He seemed confused as to why I did this. I just said that I didn't want the stall horn to be broadcast on the radio.

He also performed strangely on other flights. Since I was Assistant Chief, I began performing most of the student stage checks. There was a good excuse for this: the FAA was making big changes in the regulations under which charter departments operated. This would necessitate having a new company manual describing all the regulations and procedures.

Henry declared that he could create one very easily, so he spent his days doing this until nearly the deadline. In addition, he wrote a new manual for the flight school. He didn't show them to anyone before submitting them to the FAA, and they both were immediately rejected. The books didn't follow the regulations.

As a result, Henry got fired when he didn't show up for a scheduled flight. Our new general manager, who took over after a succession of brief stints by other men, took over as chief pilot.

John had worked for SBA some years before and was very familiar with the charter department. He also cancelled our approved school status, because Henry had not applied for renewal. I was dismayed. I was working with several advanced students who were depending on the 190-hour Commercial course. I was also working with two men studying under the GI bill, which paid for 90% of their training past the private pilot and required that they be in an FAA Part 141 Approved School program.

Eventually—not too long, really—we got that all sorted out. I was appointed to be Chief Flight Instructor, but I didn't have the experience required to serve in that capacity for the advanced courses. Another former SBA employee who was flying as the pilot for a private employer served as Chief of those courses until I had enough experience.

After being promoted to Chief Flight Instructor for SBA, I was required to have a standardization check conducted by one of the FAA inspectors. Either it happened without notice, or the plane I'd planned to fly wasn't available for some reason; I was scheduled in a brand new Sundowner, a simple 180-horsepower Beechcraft. I peered at the cockpit, and it looked familiar except for the fact that knots and miles per hour had traded positions on the airspeed indicator—no big thing.

The first thing an inspector wants to see, after the weight and balance calculation for the particular flight, is a preflight inspection. Oh my, something was odd. I took out the fuel tester, and it looked different. Usually, it was a long transparent plastic cylinder. You would use it to collect a fuel sample and look at the fuel to be sure it was the right color and there wasn't any water in it. Fuel and water separate distinctly, and different grades of aviation fuel are different colors.

This tester was unfamiliar. How embarrassing when I looked at the underside of the wing and saw that the usual access to the fuel wasn't there.

What to do? I really had no choice. I had to admit that I hadn't flown this airplane before and that it apparently had a new feature. Fortunately, a pilot is supposed to have a checklist in hand while preflighting. Since this plane was brand new, it didn't have its own checklist separate from the owner's manual, which goes into more detail. So I had the manual in hand, and I found the section that showed the new technique. It worked out all right.

This reminds me of the other time, years before, when I hadn't done my homework on the airplane I was to fly. My friend Jan and her husband owned two leaseback planes at Apollo, but Jan, the only pilot in the family, really wanted a Bonanza. I'd let her fly mine from the left seat, and she loved the performance, which was considerably more impressive than the Cherokee 180 and 235 models they owned.

She talked her husband into a demonstration flight. That's a freebie usually conducted by a salesperson in hopes that the person will want to buy a plane. The demo was set up to coincide with a little party at the airport for Beech Aero Club members. Jan and her husband were social members of the club; they came for the parties, not to fly the planes. This was early in my BAC stint and the members, nearly all male, were still sizing me up.

So the brand new Bonanza was parked on the ramp right outside the door of the club room, near the tables, which were arranged for a nice evening meal. The members watched as I showed the Edmonds the preflight and we three climbed aboard. As I went through the checklist, starting the plane, I glanced at the radios. They were not either of the brands with which I was familiar— Narco in Pipers or King in Beechcraft. Instead, there was a cluster of lovely Collins products.

They were lovely, but different. Why were there two frequencies showing at once on each radio? What purpose did the toggle switches serve? I knew I had only a hundred feet or so to go before making a fool of myself. I could taxi to, but not onto, the taxiway before having to call the tower.

I really, really did not want to have to admit that I didn't know how to use the equipment in the plane I was demonstrating. Luckily, I figured it out in those available seconds. "Santa Barbara Ground, Bonanza 17846 at SBA, taxi for takeoff with Bravo."

I experienced a silent sigh of relief as I heard, loud and clear, "Bonanza 846, Santa Barbara Ground, taxi to Runway 15 Left."

And then I flew this lovely new Bonanza around the area. I asked for Runway 25 upon returning so that the BAC members could see how nice it looked on approach and landing.

They were impressed. I could see it in their eyes when we returned to the ramp. They didn't know, and I didn't tell them right then, that a Bonanza is a beauty to land. It is very forgiving and allows picture-perfect arrivals every time in the hands of a competent pilot. The onlookers just thought that I was amazingly good, the landing was so pretty.

Jan and Dick didn't buy a Bonanza; it was more expensive than they wanted to pay. But I did get to fly with the person who bought N17846, and it was always a joy to fly.

~~~~~~~~~~~~~~~

A few foreign students came to SBA to learn to fly, often because of ads that had been placed in flying magazines years ago, when quite a few students were enrolled. The school had visa-issuing authority, and a person who was a full-time student at an approved flight school could be in the US as long as the course was being actively pursued. They were supposed to be fluent in English, which is the international aviation language—the language which must be spoken at all Air Traffic Control facilities. But sometimes the cultural differences, as well as trying to communicate in a language which was perhaps halting, made for confusion.

There was a young man from Nigeria who flew fairly well and had soloed. He sometimes got confused about directions in the traffic pattern, and I was called by the tower a couple of times about this. I took him to the tower cab so that he would understand better how it worked and also get to meet some of the controllers. He seemed quite awed by the experience. As we left, I asked him what he thought. He said, "They can see the airplanes."

His confusion about directions persisted, so I talked to him again and asked if he was left-handed. He said, "No... Yes."

I asked which it was, no or yes, and he said in Nigeria it was not permitted to be left-handed. That explained it. Forcing a child to use the non-dominant hand can cause this difficulty. We worked on it, but he didn't complete the course.

European students had an easier time; they usually were pretty fluent in English, and their customs were more similar to ours. Carl was a good example. He was from Norway and lived with his uncle while pursuing his aviation credentials. He was fun to fly with. Later, when he became a flight instructor, he was also fun to work with. Eventually, he went back home and got a job flying for SAS (Scandinavian Airline Systems).

We had a number of people from South America, and they did well, too, although sometimes little language mistakes could be confusing. One young woman from Brazil insisted on talking about being worried that the plane might dolphin. The term is porpoise. Planes sometimes porpoise if they are being asked to land at too high a speed and power complicates the problem; it's easy to get out of synch. The solution, however, is simple: go around. This is the answer to almost any problems encountered during an approach to landing.

The language difficulties were more pronounced for Asian students, unless they were very fluent in English. I worked with one young man from Japan who earned his instrument, commercial, and flight instructor certificates with me. He was very good with rote memorization, but since the FAA designated examiner with whom he would take his CFI checkride insisted that he should know what every word meant in the "How to Be an Instructor" book, I had to go over every sentence with him. Some of the psychological obstacles to learning just didn't ring a bell with him. He insisted that in Japan there was no such thing as repression, for example.

He was a hard worker, and I enjoyed instructing him. I had warned him that he could work at the school but only with Japanese students. Also, he needed to talk to them in English, using his native language only to clarify the occasional concept.

He did this for a short time, but then he found a job with a company not too far away that trained only Japanese students. He would bring his students to Santa Barbara on cross-country flights. I noticed that, unlike what I had taught him, he was very stern with his students. That was what they expected; it was the culture talking again.

Chapter 13

Women, Communications, and Other Noise

"No. I just wanted to fly airplanes."

—Jackie Parker, asked if she pursued her flying career because she viewed herself as blazing trails for other women. Jackie was the first female in a number of traditionally male USAF assignments. She was Reese AFB's first T-38 instructor pilot, the first female graduate of the USAF Test Pilot School, and the first woman in the United States to be assigned to an F-16 fighter squadron.

When I was first a flight instructor, being female had more disadvantages than advantages. There were so few of us that many people hadn't encountered one. If they did encounter a female flight instructor and didn't like her, then they were quick to report this and further the opinion that a woman's place is in the kitchen.

I have mentioned how it took an actual viewable demonstration of my pretty landing in front of Beech Aero Club members to boost my reputation. Another example was a nice young man who had seen me land my Bonanza one day and told me that he was inspired because of it. I asked him if he decided that if I could do it, then surely he, a man, could too. He had the grace to blush and deny that that's what he meant, but obviously I'd gotten it right. I softened a bit and told him that Bonanzas are very user friendly and it's hard to make an ugly landing in one. But still, it took visual proof.

Word of mouth is the best advertising, in my opinion, both for businesses and individuals. As I worked as a flight instructor, I was happy to find that people were asking for me. My schedule filled up, and before long, I had more work than I wanted. I would pass the overflow on to colleagues; it was nice to be able to pick and choose.

There was an unusual guy who flew once with my friend Marilyn across the field. He said he was opposed to any abuse of animals and insisted that she take off her shoes and not wear her leather jacket nor take her leather flight bag along. She complied, but she told me about it. Then he appeared at SBA and chose tiny, young Debbie. She was frightened and didn't want to comply. I supported her decision, and he finally went away.

Another uncomfortable situation we had to deal with was students thinking they had fallen in love with us. It's an occupational hazard, almost like the transference that can occur in psychiatry.

And then there are the students who just make passes. One of my fellow female instructors who didn't consider herself very feminine—more like "one of the boys"—told me that one of her students had flirted with her. She hadn't had that experience before. I told her to say no and, if that didn't work, to laugh. That almost always stops it.

Once, as I was walking from one SBA building to another with a very self-confident male student, he made some remarks about the advisability of us getting together. I don't remember what I said, but as we approached the other building, he said, "In that short walk, you've told me that you're not interested and never will be. I've never been turned down so efficiently before." Dating and the instructional setting don't mix, in my opinion.

Later, when I had my own school, I told the young instructors that they were not to date the students. If they really wanted to have a romantic relationship with a student, then they needed to pass that student on to another CFI.

There are lots of attractive people learning to fly and instructing, and they are aware of each other. After completing a stage check with a young woman, I told her that I wanted to see her push the airplane into position at the tie down. She caught the eye of a male instructor and asked him to help her.

I told her that wasn't the way to do it. What was she going to do when she was on a solo cross-country and there was nobody around to do it for her? Then I showed her how to do it and had her do it also.

Little training airplanes are very light and maneuverable. By the time a person gets into a plane that's heavy enough to be difficult to move, they can usually be "driven" straight in.

By the way, the young lady I just mentioned married her flight instructor. Yes, it's true: I'm not always right.

Another student and instructor fell in love and planned to get married, but it fell through just before the wedding. The male instructor, one of my employees, told me the sad news and added, "I know; you told me not to date the students."

~~~~~~~~~~~~~

"Sam" and "Claire" were a married couple who learned to fly together. Actually, although they thought they would learn together, that really isn't an option. Each person has to experience each new thing him/herself. We let people ride along on each other's lessons, available back seats and weight and balance allowing. Small things can be learned in this way, and it's fun. But any pair of students is a probable contest in the making.

To prevent competition, I assigned Sam to one instructor and Claire to another. Likewise, each learned in a different model of plane.

At first, I think they felt that I was just being difficult. Surely it would be best to have the same teacher and airplane. When I asked that they do it for the sake of their marriage, they hesitated, viewed my unwavering look, and agreed. I think—I hope—that later they understood.

Without intending it, people compete. Who soloed sooner? Who passed the written test? Who earned the private pilot certificate first?

Sam was a good stick. He worked construction, which makes for the very most apt students. Only a 17- to 19-year-old boy can beat a person who already is adept at moving all of his arms and legs differently at the same time to achieve the correct result. An 18-year-old backhoe operator would be the ideal. Sam soloed quickly but flunked the written test.

Claire was book-smart. She struggled through learning to coordinate the airplane but whizzed through the written test.

Since they flew different airplanes, Claire could blame the plane for her slow progress. Since they had different instructors, Sam could blame his teacher for his battles with the theory. So it evened out, and they both passed their checkrides at about the same time.

After that came the really tricky part. They would take trips together. That's a logical plan but not as easy as it would seem. I invited them into my office and explained the problem: someone needed to be in charge of each flight segment.

They nodded. Although the plane's controls can all be accessed from the right, it is surprisingly different to do so. Making that transition is one of the hurdles that need to be crossed when training to become a flight instructor.

Sam and Claire didn't plan to do any flying from the right seat. So what problem was I suggesting? Well, as commercial pilots know, there is always a captain, and if another pilot is involved, he/she is the copilot. The captain is in charge. The decision Sam and Claire needed to make was whether one of them would be the single pilot on each flight, or if the non-flying person would be the copilot. The duty of the copilot would be to handle the communications. Either choice works fine.

They opted for the flying pilot to do everything, except for watching for traffic. That's something any sighted person can—and should—do when sitting in the right seat. This plan worked fine for them and maybe still does.

It didn't make sense to "Les," a friend of mine who was working local control in the tower one day while Sam was flying with Claire in the right seat. They had both recently checked out in a Cessna 182, a larger and more powerful aircraft than they had previously flown.

Les had just arrived at the local position and was familiarizing himself with the inbound traffic. When Sam checked in from approach control to local, he correctly called himself Cessna 54321. However, there are many models of Cessnas, each with a different approach speed. The controller needed to know which one Sam was flying in order to sequence the traffic efficiently.

Therefore, the request from the tower: "Say type airplane."

That remark didn't resonate with Sam. Although all of our students are quite familiar with communications phrases by the time they are certified, a particular expression may not have been encountered by a pilot. There is FAA information listing these things, but Sam was the member of the couple who preferred all other aspects of aviation to studying, and this phrase doesn't surface too often.

Although Claire knew what it meant, she kept quiet because that was the strategy they had chosen. And so Sam added power and announced that he was going around. This is what confused my friend the controller, who had just repeated, "Say type airplane," when Sam didn't comply with the request.

Les was a pilot, too, and he knew that going around meant six extra minutes of flying time, which would cost one tenth of an hour of time on the Hobbs meter, which records flying time. Like many people who have been private pilots for years, he budgeted his flying costs and forgot that, as a student, he had been taught that there are two equally likely outcomes to any approach to landing: either a touchdown or a go-around.

Sam hadn't forgotten this, nor should he have, because those two outcomes never change. Every once in a while, even a very proficient pilot needs to abort the landing.

Les called and asked me to apologize to Sam, whom he didn't know, for his causing the go-around. I thanked him but reminded him that Sam did the right thing, since he didn't understand the instruction. And then I said, "When you realized that Sam was confused, why didn't you just say, 'What kind of airplane are you flying?'"

~~~~~~~~~~~~~

The local tower personnel are familiar with the training planes and are usually very patient with nervous, stammering students. It's another game at other, busier airports. One of the busiest is Van Nuys Tower in the Los Angeles area. The controllers there have a reputation of talking very fast in order to get their many, many airplanes up and down. It can be hard to get a word in edgewise.

Sometimes checkrides need to be taken at Van Nuys if an FAA inspector is to conduct the test. At the time that Marilyn and I were taking our instructor checks, we were required to do this. We would fly down to Van Nuys together for moral support.

Marilyn was first. She flew an Arrow into the busy area, took a deep breath, and at the first possible break in chatter said, "Van Nuys Tower, Arrow 12345, ten miles west with Alpha, landing, request

16Right." She said this as fast as she could and was greeted with, "Arrow 345, Van Nuys Tower, please say again slower."

Students are afraid of the tower. You can almost see them shrink when they make mistakes—and they all do.

I like a couple of ways of helping them learn that it is ok to make errors. First, when they were sufficiently out of the tunnel vision/hearing stage so that they could actually comprehend what was going on when I talked to the tower, I would purposely falter. I might ask Ground Control, "Is 504 cleared to cross 25?" even though I knew we had received that clearance call. That let the student see that such an admission didn't embarrass me, an experienced pilot, nor did the controller sound exasperated at having to repeat an instruction.

~~~~~~~~~~~~~~

Almost without exception, Air Traffic Control (ATC) communications frighten new students. Some people choose to learn to fly at an "uncontrolled" airport (an airport with no ATC) because they think this will make life easier. And it does—until they need to fly to a "controlled" airport, which they will have to do before earning the private pilot certificate. If they just want a recreational pilot certificate, they can avoid controlled airports, but that will limit them from ever using ATC.

A student who trains at an airport with local and departure controllers becomes quite sophisticated on the radio before even soloing. As with the other elements of becoming a pilot, students learn to incorporate communication into what they're doing by focusing on one thing at a time and interleaving tasks as appropriate, until they become almost second nature. Of course, it is a different story if the student is not a native English speaker. Then it's tough. We did lots of role-playing with them.

Before 9/11, it was fun to visit the tower. I made sure that each student did so, usually close to solo time. The friendly men and women who staff ATC conveyed to the student that they are just people, too.

The first time I went into the tower was the day I soloed. When I asked to taxi to the base of the tower to pick up my instructor, the ground controller said to taxi as requested and then shut down the airplane and come on up. I did, and I discovered that the excellent controller who shepherded my three times around the patch was someone with whom I was slightly acquainted in another context. It was nice to find someone from my other-than-the-airport life in the tower. I met the other folks who manned the cab that day, and they were congratulatory and made me feel proud.

Bob, the controller, was often in the local control position during my soloing sessions while working on the private certificate. He had a great voice and was always patient, cool, and helpful… until the day his younger daughter flew her first solo. He was still patient and helpful, but not so cool as usual. I had started my stint in the pattern first and was assigned to Runway 15, as was usually the case until the crosswind exceeded 10 miles per hour. At the time, the crosswind was four mph.

Then daughter began her session of three touch and goes for her first solo. Her dad's familiar beautiful voice welcomed her and assigned her to the same runway.

After her first circuit, Bob announced that the wind was now five mph at 260° and suggested that we switch to Runway 25. There's nothing wrong with that, but a five mph crosswind is very doable, and making the switch to another pattern is actually harder.

Surgeons don't operate on their family, and perhaps controllers shouldn't be shepherding their offspring on the day of first solo. When I mentioned that to Bob, he laughed and agreed that it might be true.

Air Traffic Control communications can vary from very efficient to hostile to very friendly. If it's a slow day for a good controller, there's no problem. If it is a busy day with a good controller, still no problem.

What's bad is a busy day with a bad controller, and worst is any day with a controller with an attitude problem. Fortunately, this last variety is rare. I only experienced one during all my years of days flying at the Santa Barbara Airport.

I was friends with the tower chief in the mid 1980s. My office was next to the Santa Barbara Tower in the west end of the Flight Service Station (FSS). I often taught ground school classes in the east end of the FSS building.

Often, after I had dismissed my ground school class, cleaned up, checked my office for messages, and headed for my car in the parking lot, I would run into Jim, the tower chief. I learned that he was leaving after all the other people in the tower had gone home, because he would stay after hours in order to make communications easier for the late-departing United flight. It was a small thing: he just needed to read the canned clearance (the same one every night), clear the plane for takeoff, and switch him to LA Center. But it meant a savings of time and effort for the pilots. I don't think Jim bothered to tell anyone else about this nice deed that he performed many nights.

~~~~~~~~~~~~~~

Of course, the competence and attitude of the pilot influence the service, too. Airline pilots tend to be pleasant folks, as do most other professional pilots. While ATC people generally are very patient with student pilots, this is not necessarily true with certified pilots. The type of plane being flown is a clue that the person is no longer a struggling pupil.

Tone of voice is really important. Neutral is fine, but curt and unfriendly doesn't encourage the best service. If the controller has the choice of clearing a plane to cross the active runway quickly or letting him wait for a few arrivals and takeoffs, the friendly or neutral pilot will most likely cross sooner.

I explained this to a nice guy who used his plane for his fish-spotting business. He was a friendly guy, except that he spoke very curtly—rudely even—when talking to the tower. For some reason, he never got over it; I'd hear him on the frequency later, and the same pattern continued. It was too bad, because he demonstrated all his other excellent pilot skills and instrument proficiency whenever we did his checks.

Sometimes ATC makes incorrect assumptions. For example, I did a stage check with a man who was learning to fly in his own Bonanza. This high-performance model is not usually used by students. Even though people would come to me to teach them to fly in one, thinking I would be all for it because I was a Bonanza owner, I always advised against it because it is harder to learn in a complex plane. It takes less time to learn in a simple trainer and then transition.

Student practice is also not healthy for the high-performance plane. Learning how to glide power off is not good for a high-performance airplane's engine. The inelegant arrivals involved in learning how to land are also not beneficial to the rigging of the plane. Trainers take a lot of abuse. Furthermore, insurance is very expensive (if available at all) for student pilots in high-performance, complex aircraft.

But on this occasion, I was doing a stage check with a new pilot in a Bonanza. The flight entailed leaving the airport, doing some maneuvers in the practice area, and then a return for landing. I learned on the way out that Steve did not use a genial voice when communicating. Again, here was a nice guy who normally was courteous. However, his young instructor was reluctant to criticize this successful businessman—a bad but common mistake.

While we were flying away from the airport, I mentioned the role of tone of voice in getting helpful service. After we did the practice, I told Steve that I would handle the communicating on the way back in, so he could see how I did it.

We got more of a demonstration that I anticipated. The controller had trouble connecting my voice with this plane which, up to this point, he had only worked with a pilot with an unfriendly manner. Because of the type of plane, he assumed the pilot was a full-fledged pilot, so he was not expecting to hear another voice from that plane.

The controller asked more than once, "Now, who is this again?" It was as if I had set it up, though I hadn't. Steve got the point, and he reformed.

Another group of flyers who don't get the best service are those who begin transmitting before thinking, and start with, "Uh." You can just imagine the expression on the busy controller's face when he hears the keying of the mic, pause, "Uh," and then the rambling and poorly worded request of the person who hasn't bothered to learn the proper wording or to think through his transmission before beginning. Usually the person learned to fly at an airport without a tower.

Military controllers are the exception. They, as well as the military pilots, tend to be very matter-of-fact and terse. It could be interesting trying to convey the difference to a former military pilot who was transitioning to the civilian world of flight.

Mike fell into this category. He was young and a quick study except for the communications part. When he would speak, it was very fast and sort of robot-like—no warmth. Also, he balked at changing the phraseology he had used in the military. So, although the communications sheet I had him study called for "Santa Barbara Tower, Sierra 213PT is ready for takeoff," Mike barked, "Sierra 213PT, number 2 for takeoff."

The controller answered with, "Roger." That just means, "I heard you."

"Mike," I said, "you've just told ATC that you want to wait until that Warrior has departed. I know that that instructor gives a lot of ground instruction while the engine is running, because the instructors at that school get paid more for flight instruction than ground. So we may be sitting here for 20 minutes."

Mike knew, of course, that he would pay just as much for the airplane while it was idling as in flight. The point was made, and he followed my carefully-written guidelines from then on.

~~~~~~~~~~~~~~

The people in the tower are generally pleasant folks. One day, I took a prospective student on an introductory flight—a short, cheap jaunt designed to show how fun and doable flying is. This particular young woman was looking for the beauty and freedom of the skies and did not like the idea that we would have to deal with the tower.

"You mean we need to get permission to fly?"

"Yes, and we even need clearance to taxi."

She rolled her eyes when I picked up the microphone and said, "Santa Barbara Ground, Cessna 6565L at SBA with November, taxi for takeoff."

She softened a bit when she heard the reply, "Cessna 65L, Santa Barbara Ground, taxi to 15L. Hi, Beth, haven't talked to you in a while."

However, there are exceptions to the generally pleasant description.

On May 13, 1977, I flew the Bonanza to Long Beach with my husband on board because we were taking a cruise to Mexico. As we approached the airport, which didn't have radar, I called in and was assigned a runway and told to maintain 1000 feet AGL.

As I neared the runway, I called and asked if I was cleared. The controller said that I wasn't in sight. I told him that I was over the numbers at 1000 feet. He rather grudgingly sequenced me and eventually gave me a landing clearance.

After I landed, Ground Control gave me a number to call the tower. This happens when ATC feels that a pilot has made a serious mistake.

I called and talked to the supervisor; the offended controller didn't come to the phone. The supervisor told me that the Tower controller had said that he saw my red Bonanza well away from the airport when I reported right over it. I was in a hurry to get to the ship we were boarding, so I just said, "If you look for it in the transient parking area, you will see that Bonanza 886T is blue and white. And have a good day."

~~~~~~~~~~~~~~

There are always complaints of too much noise at airports. People buy houses under the flight path, are even warned about it by real estate agents (who are required to divulge this), and then want to change the rules after buying the house. Or better yet, they'd like to get the airport moved.

I served on the SB Noise Abatement committee and listened to the complaints, as well as the calm, accepting, appeasing voices of the airport personnel who answered the questions and demands. I would have found it difficult to be so patient.

One day, we heard about a Montecito resident who insisted that a Boeing 737 airline jet was flying right over her house at about 1000 feet. When an airport person came to witness this unlikely event, the resident said that the pilot must have heard that the airport person was coming and flown higher by thousands of feet just that one day.

Of course, airlines don't fly 1000 feet above the ground. They aren't trying to annoy people, and airplanes burn much less fuel at high altitudes.

Sometimes, one person would call the Noise Abatement Hotline many times a month, airing grievance after grievance.

Amazingly, a plan was hatched to provide insulation for mobile homes near the airport. Even more amazingly, when the funding was approved, none of the owners opted to take advantage of the offer. It would be too inconvenient during the installation.

One way to address noise concerns was to adopt curfews at some airports. This was not a popular approach, at least among pilots.

My friend Marilyn chose Santa Monica for a night cross-country right after, unbeknownst to her, the airport imposed a curfew. She and her student landed shortly before the witching hour (eleven o'clock p.m.), spent a few minutes discussing the next leg of the flight, and started the engine. Almost immediately, an airport patrol officer pulled up to the plane and motioned that he wanted to talk to the occupants. He told them that they couldn't take off because of the new rule.

Marilyn mentioned that the curfew hadn't been published as a notam, which is a Notice to Airmen, and should be included in the weather briefing that pilots get from Flight Service before flying. She asked if there was any way they could go but was told that only an emergency would allow it.

She replied that there was indeed an emergency: "If I don't go home tonight, my husband is going to kill me!"

Since it was such a recently imposed curfew, the officer laughed and allowed the flight to proceed.

Chapter 14

New Beginnings

In the summer of 1983, I knew that I wanted to start my own business. I was torn between a bookstore and a flight school. I attended a training course that dealt with the ins and outs of bookselling. I found a location that I thought would be viable, and I nearly did it. But I really wanted to stay at the airport.

I was concerned about leaving one flight school and going into competition by starting my own. Luckily, I was fired that fall.

My boss had called me in a week before for an evaluation. He asked for my thoughts about how I was doing; I had anticipated this and had made a list of my accomplishments and the growth of the flight school. He didn't deny that I had accomplished a lot and that the school and I had an excellent reputation. He remarked that he had heard that I was looking around at other positions. I answered that everyone was always looking around.

A few days later, the boss called me in again and said that he had decided to eliminate my position. It was not a pleasant experience.

I put in a call to the Flight Standards District Office in Van Nuys because FAA-approved chief flight instructors are required to report vacating the position. I was surprised that the very efficient man who was in charge of surveillance of the flight school didn't return my call.

After learning that the boss had intercepted my call, I called again. This time, I reached the inspector. He confirmed that he had received my message, expressed his concern, and added that of course everyone knew why I had been fired.

Surprised, I asked what they thought. He said that it was because of the boss's wife, who worked in the office. I had no idea that the FAA knew about minor personnel relationships.

I'd been reluctant to go into competition with SBA; I wanted to play fair. Now I had no such misgivings. Most everyone else at the airport did, though. They warned me that I should not attempt to compete with my former boss; he had a reputation for being ruthless and uncaring for the human side of things.

I listened to this advice but decided not to be concerned about it. I was fortunate to have two friends, pilots who made their livings by flying nice airplanes for non-flying owners' businesses. They both backed my enterprise, not with money, but with enthusiastic words of support.

So, in 1983, I became an entrepreneur. I started my own flight school in a very small way, but I was determined to succeed. Before I opened the door to my one room, I completed the necessary paperwork to become a legal entity. I chose the name Above All Aviation because it would appear first in alphabetical listings. The time of year was good because I was able to be included in the upcoming yellow pages. This was expensive, but I figured it would be my best form of advertising, aside from word of mouth and my reputation.

One of my former students, Gary Yant, was also my accountant and friend. He helped me set up a simple accounting system, consisting of a ledger and tax reporting forms. He also told me what would be required at the end of the year.

Initially, I was a staff of one—owner, flight instructor, receptionist, and bookkeeper—and my flight line consisted of one plane. People who owned their own planes would also come to me for Flight Reviews and Instrument Competency Checks.

A biennial flight review is required for all pilots every two years unless the person has acquired a new certificate or rating or has completed other competency checks specified in an FAA Advisory Circular. Instrument Competency Checks are required for IFR-rated pilots who haven't achieved the experience required every six months. I also worked with a man who owned a Grumman and wanted to get his instrument rating, as well as a woman who worked on her Commercial in her six-seat Piper. Before long, beginning students appeared, and another plane was added to the line.

The next addition was a second flight instructor. Debbie Dennis, who had worked with me at SBA, had told me that as soon as there was enough work for her, she would like to join me. It was a coincidence that the best person for the job was another woman.

After that, we added a part-time receptionist: my teenage son Greg. He had a few little scripts to use when answering the phone, such as, "She's flying right now; may I take a message?" and "She's at the maintenance shop; may I have her call you back?" Having just one gender of instructor made it simple. Also, we thought it amusing that we two female pilots were supported by a male office staff.

Of course, that changed. Most of the succeeding instructors were men. In fact, there were only three other women during all the nearly 20 years I had the school. I did like having male receptionists, later office managers. They never got their feelings hurt or cried. To be fair, neither did about half of the girls.

I liked hiring college students for part-time office help. For full-time office managers, I liked to hire recent graduates who were trying to figure out what to do with their lives. They were bright and learned the job quickly.

Yes, there was a lot of turnover, but they were easy to train. I rewarded them with good references, and the job sounded more impressive than it was: office manager, flight scheduler, maintenance coordinator, bookkeeper, etc.

Gradually, we acquired more airplanes. Several pilots put their personal planes on leaseback with us. They had heard that they could make money that way, and if they talked to other flight schools, they were assured that they would.

I was always honest, telling them that the only people who made money that way were mechanics who could save a lot of cash by performing the required service. We did have several leasebacks owned by a local mechanic, but for others, the best they could hope for was a little help with expenses. Some costs are fixed, such as the expensive insurance for rental airplanes. However, many more vary with the amount of time the planes fly.

Some items are pricey, such as the 100-hour inspections required for school aircraft. Still, we had as many as thirteen airplanes at a time on our line over the years, including several twins.

Every few months, we would have an event: taking several airplanes to airshows and fly-ins, holding contests such as poker-runs and flour bombing contests, a party at my house. I advertised these opportunities by writing up a newsletter and giving them to people who visited the school and mailing them to others. Each issue also celebrated recent solos and earned certificates and ratings.

~~~~~~~~~~~~

One very popular type of event was an airshow. Pilots love them, and so do other aviation enthusiasts. Sometimes they were close enough—an hour or two of driving.

Every year, there was a military show at Pt. Mugu Naval Base or Vandenberg Air Force Base. These were opportunities to see expert military performances. The Blue Angels always drew huge crowds. Although the crack aerobatics teams weren't always performing, there were plenty of interesting activities.

Other airports hosted smaller fly-ins, which often included airshows. Sometimes it would be a noncommercial airline airport, and they would allow for people who flew there to sleep under the wings in the sleeping bags we brought. Some people would bring small tents. It was necessary to arrive before and leave after scheduled shows.

These performances ranged from antique airplanes flying around the pattern to aerobatic programs. A lot of time was spent just walking the rows of parked airplanes and visiting with their owners. The antique planes were usually parked in a designated area, and their owner pilots loved to show them off.

Many years, Santa Barbara Airport held an Airport Day. I was usually on the committee that planned it. We would hire a few aerobatic acts—mostly solos, although sometimes it would be a group of biplanes, for example. Margi, who learned to fly at my school and worked in our office, appeared with her group of Stearman biplanes as a wingwalker. I was in charge of airplane rides, and my flight instructors and sometimes those from other schools would give rides. Occasionally, a helicopter instructor would also offer short jaunts.

We would entice the owners of interesting old airplanes to fly them in, offering the lure of free fuel, a free dinner at a hangar on Friday evening, and free hotel rooms. We were able to do that because of donations from local businesses and charging a reasonable fee for entrance on Saturday and Sunday.

The dinner on Friday night was free to the enticees and local airport VIPs. I always got tickets for any of my pilots who participated. It was a fun event.

During the show, the airspace around the airport was closed to all traffic except for participating acts, planes offering rides, and scheduled airline flights. There was good coordination between Santa Barbara Tower and the Air Boss who was in charge of the airshow. At the end, when the airspace was again open, we would stay and watch all the antiques depart.

In the 70s, there were two-day events sponsored by a service club, benefitting charities. The main event was airplane rides. Airplane owners donated their planes, pilots donated their time, the service club donated the gas, and the proceeds went to a charity. The general public was invited and encouraged to take short flights around the city for a small price.

The Federal Aviation Regulations allow, with prior permission, a private pilot who has at least 200 hours of flight time to conduct such flights. I did this the first year I qualified. My 200+ hours were all accumulated in a period of less than two years; I flew frequently, keeping my skills sharp.

However, the person who assigned the flights felt that 200-hour pilots who were not able to fly very often deserved the chance to fly these flights, too. I didn't think this was wise. You need to be sharp to be able to pay attention to flying, the communications radio, and taking care of the passengers, who ranged from nervous to thrill-seekers.

These "Day in the Sky" occasions took place on the south side of the airport, and the flying was organized by the chief pilot there. The next time such an event occurred, I was working as a flight instructor on the north side of the field at Santa Barbara Aviation, and the flying was organized by SBA's chief pilot. It was again for charity, to benefit a fund set up for a young girl who had cancer. This time, nobody flew unless he/she held at least a Commercial certificate. Most of us were working professional pilots. That was a lot better; everyone could rely on the pilot doing what he/she said and being where he/she was supposed to be.

My final flight for the very busy day happened after I had thought I was finished. Our chief pilot paged "any Bonanza pilot" while looking at me, so I took it. Naturally, this was the one that involved an airsick passenger.

Oddly, it was a young man, the least likely category. He didn't get actively sick—not quite. I became aware of his problem as I started back inbound from the harbor. I called the tower and said that I had a queasy passenger; I asked for as few and as gentle turns as they could manage. I got a "present position direct, cleared to land" response. I thanked the guy and made a smooth-as-silk approach and a slick landing. Then I raced back to the ramp and let him out fast.

So, when it was my turn to organize the flight portion of Airport Days in the 1980s, I used flight instructors.

The people who take these rides are usually either children who are excited to get to fly or grownups who have an interest in aviation. Some have gone on similar flights every chance they got. There are always a few who want to play roller coaster, pushing the airplane down and then up, which gives the sensations felt on carnival rides. I would be happy to do it if the other passengers agreed; there were usually at least three sharing the ride.

Some folks are nervous about taking a ride. Sometimes they work up their nerve to do it, and sometimes they just ask questions. One fellow, who must have weighed about 350 pounds, asked if he'd have to pay extra because of his size. Since we had a Beechcraft Baron available that day, I told him he could pay the usual price but would have to wait until that plane was available. I thought it was odd that he then decided not to go.

Ken Ringer, who earned his pilot licenses at my school and then worked as a flight instructor there, never let me forget that I had disappointed him when he was a little boy. I didn't know that he had talked his mother into going for a flight. They both were my passengers. Ken very much wanted to sit in the front seat because his dream was to become a pilot. However, because of weight and balance, or because this kid was insistent—I don't remember the occasion—I put the mother in front. I was sorry when he told me about it later.

My Bonanza had a safety device called Magic Hand which, when activated, would lower the landing gear if the pilot forgot to do it upon reaching a slow speed or low power. I didn't use it because I didn't want that to happen during maneuver practice, nor did I want the airplane to perform the functions that a pilot should do.

Not everyone felt that way, which caused a small incident during a Day in the Sky event in October of 1976. The pilot who flew 86 Tango just before my second stint was a charter pilot who believed in using all the safeguards. Unknown to me, she activated the Magic Hand.

On my next flight, I had three passengers. I remember the young man in the right front seat. I remember him because as we were returning to land, I got an unsafe gear signal. I immediately told the tower that I wanted to depart the pattern and why. I headed west and assessed the problem. I had just realized that the Magic Hand was on but functioning strangely, when my right seat passenger asked if the gear had failed to descend—pretty observant.

I turned off the Magic Hand and cycled the gear. I still had an unsafe indication.

I called the FBO on their unicom frequency and asked to speak to a mechanic. Although it was a weekend, because of all the planes flying in the event, there was a mechanic standing by. I talked to him, and he thought the gear was probably ok. He suggested that I just do a really nice, slow, landing.

I contacted the tower and advised them of the situation. The controller asked if I'd like to do a flyby at tower cab altitude so they could look at the gear—a good idea.

I did that, and ATC said the gear appeared to be down. I knew that Beech made Bonanza landing gear very strong. If it was down, even if the locking mechanism wasn't engaged properly, the force of touchdown would lock it. So I made a nice landing and taxied very slowly to avoid any possibility of decreasing the weight on the gear. I taxied to the shop.

The young man in the right seat was happy to have witnessed this event. The two kids in the back were ecstatic. They knew they got a longer ride than anticipated, and they loved the flyby.

The repair was minor but needed a part to be ordered, so the plane sat on the ground until the next day, when the mechanic and I did a test flight. The gear functioned properly, as expected.

~~~~~~~~~~~~~

When I started my new flight school, I needed to make a decision whether to be an FAA-Approved Flight School or not. It's easier to run a non-approved school because there are fewer regulations to follow and little FAA paperwork to be done. However, for several reasons, I decided to go the stricter route. First, I had been a chief flight instructor at an approved school when I was at SBA, so I knew the ropes backwards and forwards. Second, being FAA-approved sounds better.

Most flight schools are not FAA-approved. Although they are then considered to be non-approved, they are not necessarily bad. The problem is that while there are some excellent ones that operate under the less stringent rules of FAR Part 61 rather than 141, there are some poor ones, too. It's hard to tell the difference, since the FAA does little to police them.

So I initiated the paperwork for qualifying for FAA Part 141 approval. I was quickly approved as a provisional school for two years, which is how it is always done. At the end of the two years, if I had complied with all the requirements and had an excellent pass/fail rate, I would be fully approved. I enjoyed advertising Above All Aviation as the only FAA Part 141 Approved Flight School in Santa Barbara.

It sounds really good and does promise high-quality instruction. In addition, there are some definite benefits for high-achieving students. For example, a person in the private pilot or the instrument curriculum can be certificated with a minimum of 35 flight hours, rather than the 40 required for non-approved schools. A commercial student who follows a very tight instrument-commercial program can earn a commercial certificate after 190 total hours, rather than 250—quite a difference.

Over the years, we always maintained FAA-approved status, and after several years, I was granted testing authority, which meant that I could conduct flight tests for our students. That meant a lot to them.

Although I was known for being tough, I was also considered fair. Plus, they knew me. I had usually done all of their stage checks, too, so they were used to me. In later years, my son Greg took over some of the Chief Flight Instructor duties, which lightened my load. He was granted testing authority, too.

~~~~~~~~~~~~~

Upon starting my school, I heard of a bunch of snide remarks about "Lavender Airways," and it was reported later that I had painted the interior pink. As a matter of fact, I did choose a slightly pinkish color, which looked white on the walls, instead of the more conventional white, which appeared as a dreary grey in that particular building.

When the first pilot I hired was Debbie, people were sure that I was prejudiced against men. No, she was simply the best available pilot for the job. She was a pretty, bubbly brunette who liked to go out and sit on the grass with her students when doing ground instruction. She acquired a great tan. Deb had worked in my department at SBA, and we were a good team. She eventually left to fly for the airlines.

A few months later, the next pilot I added was male. Of all US pilots, only about 6% are female. I don't know the percentage of female flight instructors, but it is probably similar.

I only had two other female instructors at Above All Aviation. One went through part of our training program and the other, from Switzerland, came to see me after earning her instructor ratings. She impressed me so much that I told her I would hire her when she moved to Santa Barbara.

The other instructors were either our graduates, people who formerly worked at SBA, or highly skilled pilots from other organizations who wanted to work with us.

~~~~~~~~~~~~~~~

Shortly after I opened my school, the 1984 Olympics were held in Los Angeles. Although Los Angeles was the official location, the crew teams competed at Lake Casitas, which is located between LA and Santa Barbara.

The sports medicine physician for the Italian team decided that he would like to rent our planes. We settled on a Cessna 172. This very personable man was a good pilot. He had no trouble captaining the airplane, but his communication procedures were problematic.

English is the international aviation language; all controllers and pilots are expected to be fluent in English. However, this doesn't always translate to being able to really understand and reply appropriately. I took the doctor to the Santa Barbara Control Tower, and he charmed the personnel into giving him some slack. We also practiced all the standard procedures and likely phrases. He was able to perform satisfactorily in the local area.

Then he informed me that he wanted to take some trips to visit sports medicine facilities in other places. These locations invariably were close to the busiest airports with the least patient ATC facilities.

My solution was to call those towers and warn them that he was coming, telling them that he was connected to the Olympics, was a capable pilot, and would be gone soon. This system worked pretty well. I always waited through the evening at the school, until he returned to Santa Barbara with a story of his adventures.

One mistake I made was in letting this persuasive man use my credit card to rent a car in Santa Barbara. There was some difficulty with his own, and he had advanced my business a fair amount of money to cover his expenses. This wasn't a problem, except for his belief that traffic laws are suggestions. For example, he wouldn't stop for a stop sign if there was no traffic. He also didn't believe in complying with No Parking signs.

Once he had gone back to Rome, the tickets started appearing. I explained the situation to the UCSB campus police, and they were forgiving. In addition, I still had some of his money on account because he expected to use my services in some fashion later. Once all his expenses had cleared, however, I returned his remaining funds and breathed a sigh of relief.

~~~~~~~~~~~~~

At one point, I decided to try to recruit foreign students for my flight school. Santa Barbara Aviation had done this with some success in the 70s; there were usually a few in attendance. They had previously placed ads in trade magazines and people would contact the school in response to these ads years after they had appeared.

The first step was to apply to the INS (Immigration and Naturalization Service, which has since been dissolved and its duties given to the newly formed USCIS) for the authority to issue student visas.

I found out all the rules and procedures and contacted the agency. Then I waited... and waited.

I went to Los Angeles to see if I could find out if my application was making progress; I was informed that the person who handled the applications was only available on Thursday afternoons. I tried unsuccessfully to get her telephone extension. I kept calling the main number and leaving messages.

Finally, after months of waiting, she called me. She wanted to know if I still wanted to issue visas. When I said yes, she terminated the call. I didn't even get her extension number.

So I wrote to the President of the United States.

People told me that this was a waste of time and postage, but it worked! The President didn't contact me, but one of his aides did, and within two weeks of my sending the letter, the INS woman called me. She said that she had been ordered to expedite my application, and she did.

Next, I worked at actual recruitment. I put ads in a few foreign flying magazines and got responses. We did get some students from these ads, but there never were more than a few at a time. The reason was that Santa Barbara is an expensive place to visit. Housing is scarce and pricey. I had collected information on apartments, rooms, and hostels, and I sent that data to prospective students. Later, when I had a website, I included it there.

The students we did get usually had a relative or friend with whom they could live, or they had a large budget, allowing them to enjoy the beautiful city.

Toward the end of 2000 and the beginning of 2001, the visa applicants changed. I charged a $200 down payment, which was credited to the students and available for payment when they began their courses of instruction. I had done that to ensure that people wouldn't just apply for a visa and then not show up.

It had worked fine before, but suddenly several students to whom I'd issued visas did, in fact, not show up. I don't know if they changed their minds, or if they came to the US and then just forfeited the money and stayed illegally. That was my fear. One person even announced that she hadn't received the visa and demanded another. I just had a bad feeling about it.

I reported the no-shows to the INS, but they seemed not to care. In the end, I dropped the visa-issuing program. This was several months before 9/11. I don't know that there was any connection; probably not, but it was strange.

Chapter 15

Good, Bad, and Ugly

I taught a wide variety of people how to fly. I enjoyed working with most of them. A few didn't work well with me. A very few shouldn't be pilots.

Most people who start flying lessons can learn to fly. The how-to-teach flying books all say that if the person isn't doing well, the instructor should assume that another teacher might do better and pass the student on to someone else. This often is a successful move, and I did that a couple of times.

There were a few cases where I told people that they were no longer welcome to fly at my school. None of them were my personal students, and I didn't do this lightly.

Flying is quite safe, but it is potentially dangerous. These people chose to disregard the limitations of the airplane or the FAA regulations, and not just once.

The first was a young man whose flying skills were adequate but whose judgment was not. Against the rules, which he was familiar with, he took an airplane up at night and flew to another airport without authorization, because he liked clicking the mic to make the airport lights come on. He argued that the rule was stupid, and he didn't even agree to go by the regulations from then on. That was his last flight at my school.

The most flagrant was a bright young man who was completing a post doctorate course at UCSB in science. He definitely understood the physics of flight, yet he overestimated his abilities and tried to make the airplane "try harder."

The last straw was the day he avoided crashing only because his very steep bank at slow speed turning final for landing occurred within ground effect. The simple explanation for ground effect is that it acts as a cushion when the wings are close to the ground, as if the air were being compressed. The Spruce Goose flew in ground effect. So did Wilbur and Orville.

He laughed when I talked to him about it; therefore, that was his last flight at my school.

I was amazed that both of these former students periodically came and asked if they could return as customers. I denied them several times.

Both got their private certificates at other schools. Sadly, the second man crashed a plane, causing injuries and one fatality. He had again tried to get an airplane to fly beyond its published capabilities.

~~~~~~~~~~~~~

I enjoyed flying with Tom, who came to me after earning his private pilot certificate elsewhere. His father knew I was an experienced Bonanza pilot, and he had just purchased a predecessor to the Bonanza, a straight-tailed Debonair. It flies just like a Bonanza, which is only one of the reasons I enjoyed flying with Tom.

Tom was great. He never made excuses; if he would start to tell me something and he could see me shake my head, he would continue,

"…but that's not right. What I should have said is…" and wait for my corrections.

He had been allowed some sloppy habits in his previous instruction. During our first flight together, when he was performing his takeoff roll on the left side of the runway (as nearly all students are prone to do), I asked him what he supposed was the reason that a line had been painted down the middle of the strip. He immediately got the point, and we never had that problem again.

I was Tom's instructor for several ratings, and he was always a joy to work with. He didn't make excuses, and he put his mistakes behind him.

Chuck was another good stick. Not only was he a partner in a Cessna 180, a taildragger that required excellent coordination, but he was a Stanford grad—a bright guy.

He was another rare student who was ready for the checkride before completing all the required hours. This was for his Commercial certificate, and the program required a specific number of hours in a "complex" airplane.

What a joke. His own plane was much more demanding to fly, but it didn't have retractable landing gear. So, after he knew all the Commercial maneuvers from the left seat of the Beech Sierra, which did qualify as "complex," I moved him to the right seat.

The next goal in his training was the flight instructor certificate, so learning to fly from the right seat—the flight instructor seat—was the next logical step. That's a transition that takes at least several hours before a person can be competent to begin practicing teaching.

~~~~~~~~~~~~~~

Although most reasonably intelligent folks can learn to fly, a few people just have poor instincts in the air. When we were practicing power-off approaches to landings, simulating a loss of power, one fellow routinely did just the opposite of what needed to be done. I'd pull the power and announce the engine failure; he would turn away from the runway. That is not a good idea.

Like a lot of people, he would insist that if it had been a real emergency, he would have reacted correctly. I ran into that response a lot, especially on stage checks.

Instructors tell students what to expect on a check; a simulated emergency is always going to be included. In my flight school, most students learned to fly in either a Cessna 152 or a 172. An unquestionable procedure is to apply carburetor heat any time the power is reduced below the green arc on the gauge. And yet, most students would fail to add carb heat when I would pull the throttle back to idle, announcing that, unfortunately, we'd just had an engine failure.

"I'd have done it if it were a real emergency."

My reply: "Well, if you don't do it in practice, you will turn the simulation into a real emergency because the carburetor will grow so much ice, it can't be melted."

Fortunately, it usually only took one stage check to change the student's reaction. However, occasionally a student on a solo cross-country would elect to make an emergency landing at an unscheduled airport because of a rough engine. Nearly always, if I got to talk to the student almost immediately, he or she would admit to not applying carb heat, or at least not keeping it on—even though the procedure is to add it whenever any engine roughness or loss of power occurs.

They just don't like to keep it on, because the heat induces a small loss of power, or even temporary increased roughness. We'd tell them over and over, and demonstrate it in flight many times, and lecture on the fact that if the plane is experiencing actual carburetor icing, only carb heat will melt it.

When they needed to be rescued, a flight in another airplane to the scene of the consternation was expensive, involving two instructors: one to fly each plane home. We always did it, though. You never knew for sure that carb ice or "automatic rough" induced by solo cross-country jitters was the cause. Occasionally, the plane did really need a mechanical adjustment.

Hesitating to apply carb heat, which is required to prevent icing in a low power situation or if the sky conditions were conducive to ice forming in the carburetor, was a common and correctable student error. I pretty much expected them all to make some mistake with carburetor heat on the first stage check. That's ok. Because I was an authority figure, friendly but still the boss, my corrections made an impression.

I can still remember learning something from the chief flight instructor when I was learning to fly. I was so excited when I told my instructor what I'd learned.

He quietly asked how many times I thought he had already told me the "secret." At the time, I didn't remember hearing it before.

I never forgot this incident. I told the pilots who worked for me about my experience, so they wouldn't feel bad if similar things happened when I flew with their students.

~~~~~~~~~~~~~~~

Another thing students don't like to do is lean the engine. In order to promote good fuel usage, keep the engine running smoothly, and prolong the life of the engine, it is necessary to provide the optimal mixture of gas and air. This is true for cars, too. In cars, the mixture used to be fixed at one fairly universal setting; now cars have computers to continually adjust their mixtures. In most training airplanes, there's a control called the mixture, which the pilot uses to achieve the best blend.

Learning to fly at a sea-level airport like Santa Barbara, a student will take off and land with the mixture full rich. An inexperienced flight instructor will postpone teaching the leaning procedure until cross-country training. Because early lessons involve a lot of changes of altitude and most flight within 5000 feet above sea level, it's not really crucial. However, students don't get used to the process in just a few flights.

Once I was the boss, I insisted that leaning be taught from day one of training. The traditional way of teaching the procedure is to retard the mixture control slowly until the engine starts to sound rough, and then enriching it a bit. Although this method works well, students hate this and later, passengers really hate it. It is just as efficient and, better yet, imperceptible to the ears to use the RPM gauge as a guide.

~~~~~~~~~~~~~~

The only time that I had an engine problem that I couldn't fix in flight was late in my career. I was doing a stage check with an instrument student in a well-equipped Cessna 152. We were maneuvering near Camarillo when the engine roughened. I told the student to continue his assignment, and I would play with the problem.

I tried all the possibilities: carb heat on full, mixture rich and then adjusted, primer checked in the locked position, magneto check. Nothing helped. In fact, the roughness intensified. We discontinued the maneuver and gave our sole attention to the problem.

We changed altitude and adjusted the mixture repeatedly. I kept us moving toward Camarillo, the closest airport. Finally, I called Camarillo Tower and requested a landing, advising the controller of our problem. He asked if we wanted to declare an emergency. I replied that it wasn't necessary unless we would be sequenced behind someone who might cause us to be denied an expeditious approach. We couldn't go around.

Camarillo Tower cleared us to land, present position direct. I kept us high so that if we lost all power, we would still make it. When we had the runway definitely made, we slipped to a landing.

The engine quit as we taxied off the runway, so I called for a tow to a local maintenance shop. I called my office and Greg flew to Camarillo to pick us up. And the owner, a mechanic, discovered that the plane needed a new carburetor.

~~~~~~~~~~~~~~

One day, I was scheduled to do a first stage check with a student who had just soloed. He was a businessman who had flown with one of our instructors for just a few weeks. I knew that he wanted to buy a Cessna 182, although he had never been in one. It was a logical type of plane to want. It had similar characteristics as the 152 in which he was learning to fly, except that it was much faster and could carry four adults and quite a bit of fuel.

I thought he would be very interested in getting a chance to get a ride in one, so I offered him that opportunity instead of our doing the stage check. A friend of mine was going to be flying one; the flight was for the purpose of taking pictures of another airplane.

To my surprise, "Larry" said he would rather not; he wanted to talk to me. This sounded serious; why would he turn down a perfect opportunity to see how a 182 performed?

I soon learned. It seems that Larry had started learning to fly a few years before. He had soloed and was on a solo flight to a practice area one day, practicing stalls. He induced a stall but botched the recovery.

Because of poor rudder technique, the airplane entered a spin. Larry tried to get out of the spin, but since he hadn't had any experience with spins, he fought the condition using aileron controls only. That doesn't work.

A spin causes rather rapid loss of altitude, and the student eventually gave up and prepared to die. He let go of the controls and, voila: the little plane recovered unassisted. This was not surprising to me, but it was a very welcome surprise to Larry.

That forgiving characteristic of Cessna 150s and 152s is one of the reasons why they are such great trainers. I always did spin training before soloing students, and I insisted that the instructors who worked for me did, too. Had Larry's first teacher done this, the scary experience could have been avoided; he'd have known that the plane could recover by itself, given adequate altitude. Better yet, he would have known how to use the rudder to stop the spin efficiently.

Why did he turn down the 182 ride and also postpone his stage check? He knew that the reason he had been given spin training before being allowed to solo at my school was that I insisted on it. He felt pretty confident that he would be able to get out of a spin if he ever entered one. He wanted to talk to me and be reassured that this was true. He also wanted to thank me for requiring this life-saving lesson, which isn't usually part of private pilot training.

It is kind of odd that the only training course that includes spin training is the Certified Flight Instructor curriculum. The reason is that airplanes, even training planes, are not required to have been certified for spins. Some can't even recover from spins.

Of course, we only did spins in airplanes certified for them.

~~~~~~~~~~~~~

My flight school was a favorite hangout for airport bums. On nice days (most days in Santa Barbara), people could sit outside on the grassy areas and watch the airport activities. Landings and takeoffs are endlessly fascinating events. On the rare rainy day when flying was postponed, pilots would show up in our small quarters and exchange stories.

Some years, the wildfires in California ran rampant. If there was a fire nearer Santa Barbara airport than one of the others that were set up to refuel fire tankers, people flocked to our airport to watch the action.

Sometimes, there would be a dozen planes taking their turns to be reloaded with fire retardant. These were old, noisy twin-engine beasts from an earlier era, and many pilots dreamed of flying them.

There was no shortage of pilots available for these dangerous jobs. Everyone wanted to at least ride in one. The best I could do was climb aboard for a short taxi trip.

One time, there was actually a fire on the edge of the airport. The resident tanker gave quite a show. It flew low, just as it did when fighting forest fires, diving to leave a load, climbing a little to approach for another dive. It looked like low-level aerobatics in much too big a plane for such a tiny area—quite exciting.

Chapter 16

Expansion and Other Excitement

A fter three years of running a small but well respected flight school, I had the opportunity to grow. My former boss at Santa Barbara Aviation asked to see me and suggested that we merge his flight school into mine.

I was dumbfounded. Was this a plot to get me off the field? I struggled to comprehend the sinister motive during a few sleepless nights.

Strangely, there seemed to be none. I blame my lack of comprehension on being born a girl. Girls, at least of my generation, never learned to play the business games men play. Perhaps if I had an MBA, I would know the rules. My degree in music didn't help—not even my graduate work in musicology.

Finally, I asked point blank what the reason was for the merger, which appeared to hold no strings. He said that his flight school was losing a great deal of money, and he thought I was the person who could turn flight training into a profitable business.

I knew that I could, so I agreed. We would use some of his school planes as leasebacks, and his accountant would monitor the books, which I, however, would handle.

The office I had occupied for the previous three years was too small for the increase in students and instructors, so SBA rented a corner of a hangar to me for a low price. It wasn't much for looks, but generally flight students are looking for authentic airport atmosphere, and by the time we had moved in, it looked pretty welcoming.

Long story short: my profits rose and there were no drawbacks. The students who moved from SBA to my school were pleased. They had been minor customers in an FBO, which focused on business jets, hangar rental, and refueling. At Above All Aviation, they were the main deal.

One young woman asked about the dress code. When I told her that there was none, she said that she had been told at SBA that she needed to dress better than the shorts and tees that she preferred. She was delighted to feel accepted and welcomed.

Eventually, the planes I didn't choose to buy were sold out of town, and I bought a few Cessna 152s from SBA. About that time, we saw little oversight and the books ceased to be monitored. The SBA attorney set the school up as a corporation: AAA Flyers Inc. The change benefitted my former boss, so there was no charge to me. Of course, it benefitted me, as well, although I always maintained responsibility (fiscal and otherwise) for what occurred at my school.

Were there any unexpected drawbacks? Not really, unless you consider the weather. During winter rainstorms, the hangar would flood, and water would enter my office, soaking the carpet. It was a pain, but not earthshaking. It did explain the low rental fee, however.

~~~~~~~~~~~~

The hangar was not very secure. The big doors, which were opened to move the aircraft that resided there in and out, made access to the building pretty easy. They were almost never securely locked. Once inside, it was pretty simple to penetrate the flimsy walls.

This only became a problem once, when we were broken into. One of our instructors, Dan, arrived one early morning to discover that the office had obviously been burglarized. He noted a few missing items, called me and the police, and handled the press, which soon arrived.

We took inventory and discovered that the main items stolen were instructors' headsets and intercoms. The total loss was about $1000.

What happened next was amazing. The UCSB police handled the case. It turned out that three students had robbed three different places that had made them angry. One stole musical instruments at UCSB, the second was furious at a relative, and the third targeted Above All Aviation. When apprehended, he announced that he didn't like the flight instructor who he had flown with.

Rob, the instructor, was Mr. All American Nice Guy; everyone else liked him. The police informed the culprit that it didn't matter how he felt about a person; he had no right to steal.

The method of catching the perpetrators was clever. The first one stole musical instruments out of lockers. Guessing that he was likely to try to sell them quickly, the policewoman visited the music stores in the area, enlisting their help.

Sure enough, the crook tried to sell to one of them, and the owner turned him in. He implicated the other two, and they were prosecuted.

Our felon agreed to pay back, a little each month, the cash to replace the items he had already sold. Ten or twenty dollars at a time, eventually we got most of the money he owed us.

~~~~~~~~~~~~~

Three times while my business was in operation, the Santa Barbara Airport was flooded and flooded badly. Airplane operations were suspended for days. The year 1995 brought the single highest daily rainfall totals, and 1998 brought the record annual rainfall accumulation. The January 1995 flood was a complete surprise; supposedly it was a 100-year event. I say "supposedly" because it happened again two months later and then once more in 1998.

Santa Barbara, although it lies along the Pacific Ocean, is desert land. Most of the lush greenery which abounds is either succulents or irrigated.

Much of the time, the area is burdened with droughts; rain is scarce. Occasionally, flooding rains occur. According to the Santa Barbara County Public Works Department, flood years included 1914, 1941, 1948, 1969, 1978, 1983, 1992, 1995, and 1998.

I woke up one morning in early January of 1995 to the realization that a whole lot of rain had fallen. My house wasn't a problem; it was located on high ground. But I wondered about the airport and checked the ATIS by phone to learn that the airport was closed due to flooding. The local TV station was broadcasting flood news.

Calling Santa Barbara Control Tower by telephone seemed my best option for checking on my business assets. Although Approach Control was monitoring overflying air traffic, most of the Tower personnel had plenty of time to visit with me. I asked if they could see my little planes and was told, "Yes, they are right where they belong, except that they are sitting in water up above their wheels."

Yikes! I had to get to the airport. My son Greg's truck seemed a better option than my Honda sedan. We drove west, one freeway exit farther than the one we usually used, because that one was flooded. We were able to get within a mile of our office and waded the rest of the way, shoes off, pants rolled up. Later, we bought rubber boots and wore them for a couple of days.

Not only did our ramp look like a lake, all the runways and taxiways did, too. What a weird sight, neat rows of airplanes all tied down but moving in the water as the wind dictated. They were safe; they all moved the same direction and not very far because they were restrained by the ropes.

Knowing that we only had a day or so before the wheel bearings would freeze, I contacted the maintenance shop that serviced our planes, as well as the pilot/mechanic next door, who was grounded like the rest of us. They both agreed to work on as many planes as they could before the water damage worsened with time and would require replacing the remaining bearings.

Before long, the flight instructors came by to check out the airport. We all decided to move the fleet across the parallel runways to Stratman Aero, the maintenance facility we used. It was on slightly higher ground. Don Stratman and his mechanic employees bunched the planes parked there close together, making room for ours.

I called the control tower and asked if we could taxi the airplanes via the access road used by fuel trucks. They didn't care; no air traffic would be affected. So we taxied slowly on the wet pavement. When we moved the couple of low-winged planes, one person taxied and two others walked alongside the wings to be sure that they cleared signs along the way.

For several days, the airfield remained closed. After the water receded, the mud that was left caused a big mess.

Gradually, the pavement was cleared, first the long runway and the taxiways that commercial airlines used. Eventually, the other runways and taxiways were cleaned, as well, and we were back in business—sort of. The office had been flooded as well. As much as a foot of water had taken residence for a while.

Aside from the carpet, there wasn't much permanent damage. Because the building was prone to flooding, the instructors kept their equipment on their desks when rain was imminent. My tiny private office was a few inches higher than the rest of the building, giving me false security. Some of my papers acquired the odor of mold.

Read more about flooding at Santa Barbara Airport in the online appendix: http://www.awomansplaceisinthecockpit.com/appendix

~~~~~~~~~~~~~

The next time, Greg and I were ready. We had discovered that we could get a reliable indication of flooding from the water level in the ditches that bordered the road adjacent to our section of the airport. When we spotted the danger level, we raced to the Airport Offices and alerted the personnel, who were about to leave on a late Friday afternoon for the weekend. Then we stopped at Stratman Aero and told Don Stratman that we'd like to bring the planes back to his higher ground.

He agreed somewhat reluctantly, thinking we were overly pessimistic. However, some of "our" planes were owned by him, on leaseback to us, and he was as eager as we to make sure they didn't get flooded again.

He helped us secure the visitors, and we managed to have them all moved by the time the water began to flood our ramp again.

From that day on, whenever the weather turned rainy, Don would ask me if I had "that feeling" again. I didn't, except for one more time in 1998, when the airport flooded again. That time, too, we rescued our little fleet in time.

Water in California is an issue of irony. At times, it is dreaded for its overabundance, and yet most other times, it is cherished due to its scarcity. Santa Barbara County has suffered through both flood and drought, often within close proximity.

However, few recall that just before the flood years of 1995 and 1998, we were in a dire drought emergency. In fact, at less than 7 inches of total annual rainfall, only one other year had a lower annual rainfall total than the 1990 water year. Interestingly, Santa Barbara received more rainfall on January 10, 1995, than in the entire 1990 rain year. With Gibraltar Reservoir empty and Lake Cachuma so low that pumps were needed to supply water to the Tecolote Tunnel, mandatory conservation practices were implemented.

~~~~~~~~~~~~~~

Airplanes that reside at airports near the ocean are prone to rust. Although they are usually made of aluminum, which resists corrosion, they do gradually acquire some damage. People who buy used airplanes would always like to obtain aircraft that have been based in Arizona, but most people know that, so they are in short supply.

One way to minimize the effect of proximity to salt water is to keep planes in hangars. Wooden hangars work really well; they absorb the moisture and protect the planes. However, most available hangars are metal. They aren't as effective, although, of course, they shield the paint from the sun.

Because hangar purchase and rental are expensive, most flight schools keep their rental fleet tied down outside. Even the FBOs, who usually have hangars for rent, do this. People who are shopping for flight instruction—and students and pilots who want to show off the planes they fly—like to visit the planes and walk around them. They are easily accessed if they live outside.

Part of the required 100-hour maintenance inspections is checking for corrosion. If there are a few small affected areas, they can be treated. Eventually, though, the plane will require stripping and repainting.

I only had to have one of the aircraft I owned repainted. I chose a paint shop at a nearby airport. I had talked to people who had used their service, and they gave good recommendations.

It takes two people to take a plane to an airport and leave it there: one to fly the plane and another to pick up the first pilot. I bribed a friend with lunch.

While we were enjoying our sandwiches, the owner of the paint shop came in and, not spotting us, told his pal that I was having a school plane painted—and that no doubt my husband was paying for it. This annoyed me quite a bit, but I kept my mouth shut. (I wasn't married.)

When it was time to pick up the airplane, I took Jimmy, my mechanic friend, along so that he could have a good look at the plane. Paint shops take the control surfaces off, and there have been cases where they put them together incorrectly. I knew of a man whose plane was rigged so that input that would normally cause the plane to steer to the left actually made it turn right.

Jimmy determined that the plane was correctly reassembled, but that the paint on the belly wasn't smooth. The man who had done the painting told me that he really needed a good checklist for making sure that everything was done properly. This time I couldn't resist. Out of my mouth came, "It shouldn't be too complicated: top, bottom, left, right, front, back."

A good paint job at that time cost $5000 for a little plane like my Cessna 172. It should have looked perfect, and by the time we took it home, N80981 looked really sharp. In fact, on arrival back at Santa Barbara Airport, the plane got compliments from the tower controllers.

~~~~~~~~~~~~~~

Not long after that, one of our rental pilots—not someone we had trained, just a checkout in a Cessna 172—took three friends flying out to the Channel Islands.

We always tell people to fly high enough over water so that should the engine quit (an unlikely event), they could glide to a landing on land. It's the same as always needing to be on the lookout for an emergency landing area when flying over land. However, this man didn't do that, and he actually had the engine quit near one of the islands. He ended up in the water.

He called SB tower and gave his position, and they were rescued before long. Nobody was hurt.

I can't imagine why he only took three flotation devices; we loaned them for free. But he and his friends assessed who was the strongest swimmer, and that person got no device.

The insurance adjuster came and talked to the pilot, who admitted that he wasn't sure he replaced or secured the cover to the oil reservoir. The adjuster felt that that was the cause of the accident.

Fortunately, we had good insurance; in fact, I had recently upped the premium on this plane because I had just had it painted. Naturally, it would be the one with a fresh new paint scheme, N80981, that was lost. Airplanes that experience salt water aren't worth salvaging.

~~~~~~~~~~~~~~

Cessna 172s were the most popular airplane in the world. This was true at my flight school, too, and I needed to replace N80981.

There are always airplanes for sale, but good ones can be hard to find. It wasn't economically feasible to buy a new one, so I wanted to find one that was made during a very short range of years. This is because those planes were the most recent ones that had 150-horsepower Lycoming engines, which were good performers and very reliable.

I leaned on my mechanic friend to help me find a good one; if it was close enough, we would go and see it. The second-best option was to have a local mechanic, who was neither the owner nor had any bias in the matter, inspect the plane.

We found one, and I paid for an airline ticket for one of my instructors to go and get it. When he called me, I was concerned; had he discovered a problem?

He said, "Beth, did you know this plane is green?"

For some reason, green airplanes aren't popular. (Actually, they are mostly white; only the trim was green.) But I was interested in the mechanical fitness of the plane, and it turned out to be a really nice flying aircraft.

Chapter 17

Ground Schools

For each new certificate (such as private, commercial, and some other achievements like the instrument rating), applicants must pass a knowledge test. My policy was that students should read the regular textbook first, and then study the test questions.

I was not in favor of the ground instructors who gave classes intended to help students pass the tests, because they tended to discount any subject matter that wasn't on the test. They also liked to have their ground schools be the first thing a student would do, even before the first lesson. I heard from several people that if a student asked a question about something that wasn't covered in the class, the answer was, "You don't need to know that. It's not on the test."

One of those questions was how to handle an in-flight engine failure. You don't need to know that?

There is a lot of information that needs to be planted into a pilot's brain in order to operate safely. True, not all of the data needs to be remembered perfectly; in many situations, just knowing where to find the answer is fine. But if a person isn't at least familiar with the subject, he may not even know that the answer exists.

These ground schools intended just to pass the test tended to be held over one weekend. Needless to say, that's too much information to really learn in that length of time. A lot of trick memory aids are used. One teacher told me that he could teach most effectively to a person completely new to aviation. He cited as an example the wife of a businessman attending an instrument ground school. She came with him just for companionship, knowing nothing about flying. He had read about instrument flying, so his mind would shoot off in various directions during the presentation. She, on the other hand, absorbed the material without being distracted by associations. Just for the heck of it, both took the exam the next day. She scored better than her husband.

The exam is always scheduled for the next day. This precarious storing of knowledge fades fast; after a week or two, the students would most likely flunk the test.—not my idea of good instructional technique. The only couple of students I ever sent to one of these quickie courses were ones with test jitters that caused them to fail tests even when they knew the material. The gimmicks got them past the hurdle.

When people came to me with the test already passed and ready to begin their flight training, I'd usually find that they needed to start at the beginning with the book work. Of course, there are the exceptions; they were almost always people who did a home-study course on their own, not an accelerated ground school.

It's really more enjoyable to coordinate ground and flight instruction. It fits together nicely, and each strengthens the understanding of the other. Either instructor-supervised home study or regular instructor-taught ground schools can do this fine.

I enjoyed teaching ground school classes to our students. They would usually meet twice a week for two 3-hour sessions, adding up to 36 hours.

There would be a nice mix of students: those with some background in the subjects, and also brand new people. You know, the ones like me, who came from being a former teacher and stay-at-home mom into the foreign world of the airport. When I was training flight and ground instructors, I'd always use me as the example of the student who needed to learn the most.

In our classes, there would usually be about 8- 20 people in attendance. It was nice when they would start with the first class, but they could begin in the middle if it worked better for them. Usually, the students who began their training knowing nobody else who was learning to fly would become acquainted and enjoyed sharing experiences. Sometimes they would even go along in the backseat of each other's flight lessons.

The class would share their triumphs; a first solo was a cause for celebration, as was a conquest over the fear of performing stalls. Excitement was contagious, and everyone became more enthused as they traded stories.

Occasionally, a team would take the class, often a father/daughter or father/son combo. One man and his daughter wanted to share an activity, and since the daughter really wanted to learn to fly, they chose flight school, beginning by attending my ground school. The daughter never did become a pilot, as far as I know, but Dad did. He bought his own airplane, then another and another.

Teaching ground schools was fun, and I taught a wide variety of them. Most were small groups of students, all going for their private or instrument tickets.

My very first one was a private pilot class for the local Civil Air Patrol kids, which my friend Marilyn Weixel and I did together. I taught a college credit Commercial Pilot class at Santa Barbara City College, which was interesting. Some of the students wanted all the information they could get and asked interesting questions about subjects that weren't even in the curriculum. Others dropped out when they realized they needed to study.

Another unusual class was a perk that the City of Santa Barbara, Airport Division, gave their employees who chose to take the opportunity one year. My students ranged from people who couldn't read, up through the airport director, who was a student at my school. I really had to be a standup comic to keep some awake while giving all the information needed by the serious pupils.

I repeated this class for the benefit of people who had been unable to attend the first series and also for the airport firemen who hadn't been included the first time. Some people walked to the classroom; some drove. The firefighters who were on duty drove their huge trucks and kept their radios on.

At the end of the series of classes, each attendee was given the chance to take an introductory flight lesson. It amazed me that only a very few did this. Yet, all these folks considered me a friend afterwards, and that was nice.

Occasionally, I would teach a special class, such as an instrument flight instructor intensive class, which would take about six flight instructors through the information they needed to be able to teach future instrument students. These were fun, because I would have each person choose topics they would research and present to the rest of the group.

Once, there were several foreign students at Above All Aviation, all working on instrument ratings at about the same level. All had functional but limited English skills. I held a private class for them, covering holding patterns, the ADF, clearances, and communications—all subjects that are challenging for native English speakers and more so for others.

I worked hard to make the presentations very logical and clear. I focused on each student, trying to make sure that he was staying with me.

They were polite; they didn't want to offend me by indicating that they didn't understand my explanations. In fact, they were so polite that they didn't mention what I had been doing to my face. At the break, I visited the restroom, where I glanced at the mirror. My reflection revealed that the colors of the felt pens I had been using on the dry erase board had been transferred via my fingers (which I'd used in lieu of an eraser) to my face.

I washed my face; then, when the class reconvened, I mentioned my clownish look to the pupils. They didn't react. A lot of cultures hold teachers in high esteem, and two of these young men were from Japan, where that is definitely the norm. Other than thinking that it was odd that their teacher was a woman, they were very respectful.

The most fun class I taught was one I volunteered to do at the request of San Marcos High School, which, incidentally, was the school my children had attended. The school was helping its teachers have extra prep time for a new program they were undertaking. Each week for several weeks, the students could take a couple of hours one morning and either study or take one of a number of elective courses being presented by volunteers from the community.

I had about 20 boys and girls in my class, a private pilot ground school. At the first class, I told them that we didn't have enough hours available to do a standard 36-hour class, which was normally required to cover all the material. I gave them the choice of choosing the topics that interested them most, or moving very fast so that we could cover all the information in 24 hours. These enthusiastic kids chose to do the whole thing and promised to study hard.

That was what was so fun for me. We moved quickly, they stayed focused, and we covered it all. They were bright and asked intelligent questions, and they answered mine.

A few of these children later became pilots; I don't know how many eventually achieved that goal. At least two pursued aviation careers.

I also worked with another program for a local elementary school. Santa Barbara Airport was paired with Isla Vista Elementary School in the area's Adopt a School program. This school is unique in the area: located next to the University of California Santa Barbara campus, it has an extremely diverse makeup. The children spoke 17 different languages, and many were in programs to learn English as a second, third, or fourth tongue.

Volunteers would provide lessons on aviation to whichever group was selected in a particular year, for example, fifth graders with a high interest in the subject. I would teach one or more sessions on "How Planes Fly," or "Planning a Cross-Country," or another subject best taught by a flight or ground instructor. I wonder if any of those kids ever learned to fly. I do know that the course broadened their horizons.

I was often asked to speak to area junior high and high school students, as well as the local colleges. I was chosen because I was a woman working in an "atypical" job.

I liked doing this. My own junior high school aged daughter and her friends discussed working in a store or office, but not as the owner or manager. I felt that if my own child couldn't see that women can aspire to high goals, probably many young girls did not yet have the concept. I didn't try to influence the kids into becoming pilots; my message was that they could aim high and in unusual directions.

I was asked to speak at Santa Barbara City College during a conference on women's issues. I planned to tell my usual story: being a schoolteacher, a good but conventional choice for women, and then moving to an atypical occupation. But then the space shuttle crashed a few days before the event.

Usually, during the question and answer period, I would be asked about being an astronaut. This time, I didn't wait for that portion of my presentation. I raised the issue myself.

I can't remember what I said, but I do remember that the last question someone asked was if I would still want to go into space. I said that I would. That was followed by silence, but eventually they applauded. Several students told me afterwards that they liked my enthusiasm.

The local colleges, including UCSB, Santa Barbara City College, and Westmont College, would have career days, and people from various occupations would be asked to provide information on their fields. These events would often consist of stations, which the kids could visit according to their interests. Sometimes girls who had never considered aviation or science would stop by and learn of new options.

Also, the three local high schools had career days, which often included presentations in classrooms. I really liked doing those. I'd give a synopsis of the possible aviation-related occupations and then encourage questions.

The audience would consist of two groups: kids who knew they wanted to be either military or airline pilots, and also boys and girls who just wanted to get a little information on what was available. Again, I emphasized the idea that they should look at all the options and figure out what would be the best, most interesting options for them.

~~~~~~~~~~~~~

Another specialty group I worked with was airline pilots who needed aircraft checkouts. These pilots nearly always fell into one of two categories. First, and a joy to work with, were the adaptable ones with good skills and a modest attitude. They would urge the instructor to be watchful because they hadn't landed a little airplane in a while. Second, and no joy, were the cocky ones who assumed that, now that they were airline captains, they were invincible.

The ones with their humility intact and a lack of vanity might make an error in judging where to start the flare, but only once. They'd make a deprecatory comment, and be fine on the second attempt.

Usually, the macho guys could also make the transition to small aircraft fairly easily, but occasionally, they would cause a problem. One, a captain for one of the Mexican airlines, was an example of this. My boss assessed his demeanor and assigned him to me, the newly appointed chief flight instructor, for a checkout in a Sundowner. I told the man that I had only an hour and, though I would defer the paperwork until after the flight, the flight would have to meet the standards. All I required was private pilot standards.

We did the preflight together. It was efficient that way, as I could point out the peculiarities of the type of plane. We took off and left the pattern for some airwork, which was satisfactory. Then I reiterated that I had an appointment, so we had time for only one landing.

Pilots joke that a good landing is one that we can walk away from. In this case, we still would have been able to do so if I had not taken over when we came close to stalling just prior to landing, but the airplane would have suffered damage. So, as we returned to the FBO, I told him that he would require another flight and several landings before he could rent the plane.

He protested that all he needed was to make one landing after treating his friend to a joyride. My answer was that I had to be certain that the plane wouldn't require a trip to the maintenance shop afterwards. He walked out without paying.

I was concerned about my boss's reaction, because he was always concerned with the bottom line. When I told him what had happened, however, he was fine with it, commenting that I had done my job, which what I was being paid for.

~~~~~~~~~~~~

Because I began instructing in my thirties, I was often the choice of older pilots for their competency checks. They preferred to fly with someone a little older than the usual early-20s CFI.

It was fun flying with retired airline pilots. They had great stories to tell, and right after retirement, their skills were excellent, of course. The only glitch was that, out of habit, they would call the tower saying, "Santa Barbara Tower, American..." or "United..." and then correct themselves with a head shake of disgust.

What wasn't fun was when their skills deteriorated. Usually, they anticipated this and always asked me for comments on how their current abilities compared with the last time we flew.

Often, one of the first things to go downhill was communications. They'd start having trouble remembering clearances, so they'd make mistakes repeating them back to ATC. Sometimes, a young tower controller would let a note of condescension color his voice, and I hated that because the old pilot would hear it, too.

Occasionally, I would have to be the one to suggest that they should no longer use their instrument ratings or fly without another good pilot in the right seat. This was always sad. Even sadder was the day that the widow would bring me stacks of flying magazines after her husband's death and say that she didn't know who else would want them. In no case had one of these pilots' wives ever gone along on one of the flights.

So often, spouses don't like flying, or they're fearful, or both. I am so glad that my daughter-in-law loves to fly. She is happy that Greg is an airline pilot and has also enjoyed many trips in his Cessna 172.

Of course, it isn't only pilots of the airline variety who have mates who dislike airplanes. It happens at every level. One teenaged student pilot, who was very enthusiastic and bought lessons with his tips from his job as a waiter, had a cute little girlfriend who confided that "Joe" was keen on flying to Vegas as soon as he got his license. She said that she planned to take a bus and meet him there—not a good portent for their continuing relationship. Pilots work around their wives' preferences; girlfriends are less permanent. I warned her of that, but don't know how it turned out.

~~~~~~~~~~~~~~

About once a year, I would teach a ground school for beginning pinch hitters. Pinch hitters in the aviation world have nothing to do with baseball. Instead, they are passengers who get a little training in order to help them fly a plane should the pilot become disabled by a heart attack, stroke, or some such thing.

A full-fledged pinch hitter course involves both ground school and flight training to the point where the person could land the airplane safely, if not prettily. I always agreed to attempt to convince the potential spouse to attend the ground school. Never would I wheedle her to take a flight lesson. If she wanted to, fine.

Usually, I would hold the class as a result of several soon-to-be licensed student pilots asking if I would help convince their wives to fly with them after they were certified to take passengers. The class also included wives or girlfriends of experienced pilots.

I would start by saying that I could imagine myself in their positions if my husband had been the one to become a pilot and I was reluctant to ride with him. Then I would choose the least frightened person in the room and ask her to share her concerns.

One time, it was "Gwen," whose husband was a professional charter pilot. She said she tried to just sleep. She'd periodically wake up, look at the gauges in front of her, and if everything seemed to be within a green arc, she'd go back to sleep.

Another time, it was the wife of a poor to mediocre pilot who was brave enough to fly with him. She said all she wanted to know was what an aileron was and what the Mile High Club was.

Then I would go around the table, asking each for their thoughts. After addressing these concerns, or postponing some until we reached that area, I would give a very simple explanation of why planes fly and how they are rigged to do so on their own if they are temporarily jostled into a bad attitude.

We would have a brief session on communications, another on reading the sectional chart (a relief map with easily identifiable landmarks), and I'd go over the significance of the various gauges.

Sometimes the same day, or individually on a different day, I would take the women out to the flight line. First, I'd promise that they wouldn't have to go flying—I wouldn't even untie the planes. Pointing out the control surfaces we had already discussed, we would do a walk-around.

For wives whose husbands rented planes, I would use one of our school airplanes and let them sit in it as we looked at gauges and radios. I'd demonstrate how simple it is to talk with the tower by calling ground control and saying, "Wind check for one seven Lima, please." The prompt reply of "Wind 280 at 10" amazed them.

If the pilot had his own plane or was in a partnership, I would offer to show the wife that particular plane's controls and gadgets at another time.

One unusual case was the quite elderly wife of an equally aged pilot who owned a single-engine Cessna. The man really wanted his wife to learn how to land the plane, because his health was beginning to deteriorate. The wife really, really did not want to do this.

She and I sat in the front two seats of the plane one day, and we looked at the panel in front of us. With the glasses she was wearing, she couldn't both see the instruments and look outside into the distance. That's when I did something that the husband would not have appreciated: I told her that there was no way she could learn to fly the plane unless she did something about her vision. She teared up a little and thanked me.

Another time, I took the wife of a poor to mediocre pilot flying. She wanted to see what it was like to manipulate the controls herself.

Since her husband always had another pilot along when they flew, she never rode in a front seat. Usually in this sort of situation, I would have the mate fly from the right seat, because that's where they usually sat. This time, I put her in the left (pilot's) seat. I sat in the passenger (or flight instructor) position.

I had her do the usual maneuvers: straight and level, medium banked turns, climbs, descents. She did quite well. Then she turned to me and said, "It can't be this easy!"

I never flew with her husband, but I knew his flying reputation from other flight instructors who had experienced his piloting practices. I knew he never really learned to let the plane fly itself. He constantly made adjustments, which didn't make for a smooth ride. His wife had assumed that this was normal and that it took a lot of work to fly a little airplane.

Another wife who considered learning to fly for the usual reason—self-protection—told me that while dozing in the right seat one day, she realized that there was a recurring pattern of warmth alternating with coolness in the cockpit. She opened her eyes to find that her husband had fallen asleep and the plane was making 360s. The change in climate occurred as the plane faced into and then away from the sun.

I taught her a few skills, and then she decided that mainly she would just stay awake so that Husband would, too.

If it is the passenger who requests the training, it works out well. In that case, the only problem usually encountered is that the person only wants to learn to land. To her, that sounds economical, so it takes a little demonstration to show that it's almost impossible to perform a safe landing without first practicing the basics of level flight, turns, descents, changes in airspeed, etc.

Typically, however, it is the pilot, generally male, who wants his wife to take some pinch hitter lessons. Often, the wife is reluctant or unwilling, usually because of fear. I saw many tears caused by the determination of the pilot spouse.

One nice lady was brought to me by her rather arrogant husband. We talked about the options of joining a class or doing an individual course.

She seemed frightened, but I didn't realize the extent of her emotions until the day she came back by herself. She cried and cried as she explained that she was terrified but felt terrible about not being a good Christian wife. She felt she should be obeying the wishes of her husband as per the Bible.

Several women confided that their husbands (1) ran out of gas in their cars, (2) didn't maintain their cars well, or (3) were somewhat reckless drivers.

I knew all of these men well enough to soothe the wives' fears. They planned and preflighted thoroughly, so they wouldn't run out of fuel. They were flying the planes on my line, so they didn't have the responsibility of scheduling maintenance. I knew their flying habits to be capable and safe.

After all, poor planning in a car just results in inconvenience: having to pull over because of running out of gas, for example. That's not so handy if it happens in the sky, and these guys know that.

Of course, there are a few scary flyers around most any airport. They're too cheap to pay for good maintenance, or they don't bother to spend the extra few minutes to perform an adequate preflight. Some think it's admirably macho to scare their passengers with very steep turns. Fortunately, I was never approached for an opinion by wives of men whom I knew to be less-than-careful pilots.

Chapter 18

Decisions

O ne weekend while I was working at Santa Barbara Aviation, the SBA maintenance shop manager came to the office to ask me if I would like to fly a Cessna 170 out of a farm field near the airport. I immediately said no, although a 170, being a light taildragger, would be one of the easier planes to take off in from a rough surface.

Naturally, I was curious about the cause of the aircraft having come to rest in a vegetable patch. So I accompanied Mike, in his truck, to the site. Mike gave the little plane a quick going over; it appeared undamaged. It also appeared to have absolutely no fuel in its tanks.

I was familiar with the type of airplane and started thinking that, if the plane was fully fueled, it should have easily made it to our airport. I questioned the guy on the amount of gas he had measured during his preflight. The answer was fairly convoluted.

I asked the pilot if he had topped off the tanks, and he said yes. Then I asked if they looked completely full when he did the preflight. Eventually, it turned out that he hadn't actually looked in the tanks.

The plane was new to him, and he'd ordered it fueled but had failed to check the level.

That's bad. You never fly a plane without checking for yourself that there is adequate fuel—even an airplane with high wings, which requires standing on a little stool or ladder.

At first, I had felt a bit bad about refusing the request to fly the 170 to the airport; I was the only taildragger pilot around that Saturday. But I stopped feeling sorry once I ferreted out his negligence. Too bad it cost more to have it trucked, but you never know the condition of an unfamiliar plane sitting in someone's farm field.

The competence of the two people who made the trip was also soon shown to be in question. The passenger, the former owner of the Cessna, told me that when it became apparent that the landing would have to be short of the airport, the two men argued about whether to land with the furrows or across them. Luckily, the former option was chosen.

Then there was another guy who, also in a Cessna 170, made an emergency off-airport landing several miles from Santa Barbara Airport. He did a beautiful job, considering that his options were few and the field he selected was short and surrounded by obstacles. Several of us local pilots made trips by car to see the plane sitting intact in this very small area.

Unfortunately, the next day, he chose to add a little fuel and attempt to take off.

The liftoff was fine, but he didn't have enough altitude to clear a fence, so he turned. The plane had just enough airspeed to maintain flight in a wings level attitude; the sacrificed lift resulting from banking caused the ensuing crash. He wasn't high enough to injure himself, but the little plane suffered a fair amount of damage.

Later that day, I was listening to our general manager, an excellent pilot, describing the event to a couple of other pilots. He didn't notice the 170 owner entering the room as he continued the story of bad judgment.

When he looked up, he saw the guy and was embarrassed, but he said, "Well, you have to admit, it was a pretty stupid thing to do!"

The chastened man agreed. It would have been better to pay for trucking the plane to the airport. Little planes are amazingly easy to take apart.

~~~~~~~~~~~~~

Watching students' opinions of themselves change as they learn to fly is an unexpected bonus of teaching people to fly. I remember individuals whose bearing went from timid and reserved to confident and proud. I don't think any of these people changed badly; the ones who became offensively overconfident started out with a tendency in that direction.

The first solo flight is an extremely fulfilling milestone. It wipes that worried expression right off the student's face.

One woman student pilot was always tense, never smiling. I don't know why she was taking flying lessons, but I'm guessing it was to prove something to herself or someone else. And then, the day she soloed, she was absolutely beaming.

Fortunately, we took a picture of her while she was on her high. She flew very little after that, but she had that one great memory. She did it and she was proud.

There was a very meek young man who took his lessons very seriously, did all of his bookwork, and came prepared for each lesson but didn't say much. And then he soloed!

His gain in confidence was remarkable. By the time he achieved his private pilot certificate, he was barely recognizable as the person who took his first lesson. It just got better and better as he built more hours and earned an instrument rating. These weren't transient changes; I knew him for several years, and he never went back to being meek and mild.

On the other hand, people who are celebrities and accustomed to special attention are just regular students and customers when they take flying lessons. The Santa Barbara area—particularly Montecito—houses a bunch of celebrities, and some of them are pilots.

One, the very successful Hollywood actor Gene Hackman, owned a Bonanza. He flew well, but not often.

One day, he called me to say that someone wanted to film him flying his plane, and he was feeling rusty with his landings. (They were filming from the ground.)

I assured him that I would go along, and nobody from the ground would know the difference if I helped him a little. He agreed—he didn't have time to brush up before the filming.

When he arrived, he was nervous, but as I had assured him, he was able to make picture-perfect landings with my coaching. Any experienced flight instructor could have done the same thing.

Another time, this same actor decided to get an instrument rating. I was just starting an instrument ground school, and I told him that was the way to start, so he attended the first session. It involved some math, and he got the wrong answers.

I asked him if he had a calculator, and he didn't. I advised him to buy one. He didn't want to. I told him he could get a cheap one. Of course, that wasn't the issue. I don't remember why he didn't want one.

The next day, he stopped by and said he didn't want to attend the ground school; he wanted me to tutor him. I said I would in the evenings, but since I had young children, I told him it would have to be at my house. He agreed.

He brought his calculator, and we had a good session. Of course, a person gets better training when it is tailored just for him.

The next time we met, there were some simple math problems to solve, and he got them all right, despite not using his shiny new calculator. I mentioned this, and he said that it was because he wasn't afraid of me anymore.

I thought that was hilarious. But of course, it is hard to play the role of a student when you are a successful adult.

Robert Zemekis was another Hollywood biggie who got training at our school. He was another very nice guy who didn't let his ego get in the way of improving his proficiency.

In fact, he was even helpful. In 2001, when I got married, I had arranged for a photo shoot of Don and me, in case the pictures of the actual wedding (which would take place in small town Iowa a few weeks later) didn't turn out well. I was bemoaning the fact that it was a murky day, not sunny as I had hoped and the forecast had suggested.

Friendly Director Zemekis, certainly an authority on the subject, quietly mentioned that the day was perfect—like having a huge light box. Of course, he was right, and the pictures turned out fine.

My son Greg flew with him quite often and even received a gift of keepsakes the Christmas that *Polar Express* was released.

Another celebrity who based his planes at Santa Barbara Airport was Fess Parker. He was very recognizable because of his fame from playing Davy Crockett, and because he was so tall he was hard to miss. But he was a genuinely nice person who liked the airport atmosphere and chatted with other pilots and people who worked there.

John Travolta was another famous person who was pleasant and low keyed at the airport. He based his Citation Jet at Santa Barbara Aviation and flew it often.

A number of well-known people also arranged to take charter flights while I was working at SBA. Two examples are Bob Hope, who couldn't seem to resist telling jokes, and Julia Child, who behaved just as she did on television: happy and friendly.

In 1974, Ronald Reagan bought a 688-acre ranch called Rancho del Cielo northwest of Santa Barbara. This was during his second term as Governor of California. During Reagan's presidency, the ranch became known as the "Western White House."

This impacted Santa Barbara Airport because the ranch was very near the Gaviota VOR, which coincides with a much-used low point in the mountains between Santa Barbara and Santa Ynez. Because of its proximity to President Reagan's ranch, several thousand feet of airspace just above the area were designated as restricted airspace, which meant that aircraft were prohibited from entering it.

Planes flying IFR were monitored by ATC, and their clearances kept them from intruding. VFR traffic, however, usually changed frequencies after leaving the airport and were responsible for their own altitudes and routes.

In the early days of this new restriction, the government used casual monitoring of VFR traffic over the area, which was later replaced by precise measurement. During the early days, I flew to Santa Ynez, careful to be above the ceiling of the protected airspace. However, the person who was monitoring airplanes (just using his eyes) saw the big SBA and KIST painted on the bottom of the wings. (KIST is the name of the radio station for which I flew a traffic watch in that plane.) Since those letters were so much larger than the tail numbers that identify planes, he assumed I was flying too low.

I was reported to the FAA and called by them. Fortunately, I knew the man who questioned me about it. I explained what plane I had been flying and that I had been very careful to be well above the limit. Because I had a good reputation, he accepted my honest statement and the matter was dropped.

In 1983, Queen Elizabeth II and Prince Philip made an official visit to Santa Barbara as part of a tour of the western United States. The Queen had planned to sail on her yacht *Britannia* from Long Beach Harbor, but a massive storm prevented the ship from leaving port. Instead, she flew into Santa Barbara Airport, where she was greeted by President Reagan.

Because the weather was so bad, the airplane was towed inside a huge hangar and the festivities occurred there. We had a great view of all this from the south windows of Santa Barbara Aviation. We weren't doing any flying that day anyway.

~~~~~~~~~~~~~

All flight instructors have Commercial certificates, which allow them to do other kinds of flying, and we sometimes got requests for non-instructional flights. Scenic flights were popular because Santa Barbara is a beautiful area, with mountains to the north and ocean to the south. After Michael Jackson built his famous house with the carousel, which was easily seen from above during a quick flight from Santa Barbara, people would like to fly over it. At certain times of the year, the lush fields of flowers that were grown north of the mountains were a beautiful sight. Some people just wanted to see their houses from above, and others gave a gift of a local flight to a friend or relative.

Every now and then, someone would ask for an unusual experience with an airplane. Our Arrow was requested as a backdrop for a photo shoot for advertising by a national chain of men's and women's clothing. Another time, one of our Cessnas was featured in an episode of a television series in which the female star played a pilot; it had something to do with wild animals.

A different ad campaign was for a company that sold wind surfers. For this ad, I ran the engine of a plane, creating wind so that it looked as if the craft was on the ocean.

Another time, "Good Morning, America" shot a segment on my flight school's ramp, interviewing one of our students and following his progress around the traffic pattern with a camera.

When people have opted for cremation after their death, they often have chosen a burial at sea. This requires an authorization, but the funeral home would arrange this for their clients. Sometimes we would be asked to perform this service. Someone from the mortuary would deliver the cremated remains, which arrived in a plain brown box that held the plastic bag containing the remains. One of our pilots would fly at least three miles offshore and then consign the contents to the ocean.

At times, there would be nobody from the surviving family who wanted to witness the flight; about equally frequently, there would. People could go along on the flight if they chose, or they could watch from the ground.

If there was a group of people, they would often get together at Goleta Beach, where they could see the airplane. We would tell them what time to expect the plane to take off, and they would know what the plane would look like. Then they could look up and see the aircraft cross the coastline, wag its wings at them, and watch it fly south. Sometimes on a clear day, they could see the ashes flutter to the earth. One time, the mother of the deceased saw the sun hit them and they appeared to be pieces of gold.

One or more people could go along on the flight, depending on the size of airplane they had reserved. They could choose to release the remains themselves, but usually it was better if the pilot did it. Not all of the pilots wanted to do the flight, but there was always at least one who did, and that person tended to be one who felt honored to be able to perform this service for the family.

~~~~~~~~~~~~~

Sometimes, we have to face the fact that aviation isn't the safest career. For the passenger, it is statistically a very safe mode of travel. However, for pilots who fly nearly every day, death sometimes comes early. So I have attended several memorial services for professional pilots who died before natural causes would have felled them.

It's always a celebration. Old pilot friends appear from far and wide. Lots of reminiscing occurs. Usually the family reads the poem

"High Flight," which they thought only their pilot loved one knew. Still, it's very moving in that circumstance, and it speaks to us all.

High Flight

Oh! I have slipped the surly bonds of Earth
And danced the skies on laughter-silvered wings;
Sunward I've climbed, and joined the tumbling mirth
Of sun-split clouds, — and done a hundred things
You have not dreamed of — wheeled and soared and swung
High in the sunlit silence. Hov'ring there,
I've chased the shouting wind along, and flung
My eager craft through footless halls of air...
Up, up the long, delirious burning blue
I've topped the wind-swept heights with easy grace
Where never lark, or ever eagle flew —
And, while with silent, lifting mind I've trod
The high untrespassed sanctity of space,
Put out my hand, and touched the face of God.
— John Gillespie Magee, Jr.

Copyright status of "High Flight" is in the online appendix: http://www.awomansplaceisinthecockpit.com/appendix

Epilogue

I wrote much of the content of this book in the 1990s, while I was enjoying my aviation adventures. It was only after I retired from flying that I got serious about it as a book, looking at it again from the perspective of my new, delightful world.

My life took an unexpected and lovely fork in the road in 2000, when I became reacquainted with my high school sweetheart, Don Niebuhr. When we were dating at sixteen and seventeen years of age, we had wonderful times together... punctuated by many disagreements.

While we could spend hours talking about anything and everything—past, present and future—we were strong personalities and would sometimes clash. The last time that happened, we started dating others. We both regretted our breakup, but we were also both quite stubborn.

We each got married and raised families. Our paths seldom crossed. Don continued to live in Iowa, while I moved to California shortly after graduating from college. We saw each other briefly at the occasional high school class reunion, but that was about all.

That is, we seldom crossed paths until we both agreed to serve on the committee for our 2002 class get-together.

Our class had reunions every five years, and Don had attended all of them. I had missed most, and it was fun to reconnect with class-mates to plan the event. I still lived in California but flew back to Iowa to help—it was just a quick airline flight to Denver, followed by an-other to Des Moines. This was easy for me to do, because I charged all the fuel for my flight school airplanes to my personal credit card, so I had earned a bunch of Frequent Flyer miles.

While I was in town, Don invited me to have dinner with him. Conveniently, both of us were single, and we found that we still had a lot to talk about. Just as when we were kids, we enjoyed chatting about almost anything.

When we first embraced, I remarked on that fact that he smelled so good! I'd forgotten, but it came right back. It felt good to be back in his arms after all those years.

As we continued to see each other every few weeks, we found that we were quite compatible. We walked into an art gallery and both chose the same painting as our favorite. Delighted, we tried it again, and the same thing happened. We were careful not to give away what we favored so that we wouldn't influence each other.

Both of us being musically inclined, we were pleased to find that our taste had developed similarly there, too. It was the same with mu-sicals and plays.

What fun! Later, when we built our new house, it was a delightful experience because, again, we had the same taste. The little chores of selecting tile, paint, and eventually furniture and art pieces were just plain fun. Many of the vendors we dealt with told us that such deci-sions often took couples to the brink of divorce.

We were done with fighting. Oh, we had the occasional squabble at first, but nothing serious. It was nice to discover that we had actually become grownups, rather than bickering teens.

We decided that we wanted to spend the rest of lives together. Not being youngsters, we were married the next year. It wasn't like getting to know a stranger. Although we hadn't kept up contact, we had graduated from a small high school and would have known if one of us was an ax murderer.

Because Don had retired, he moved to Santa Barbara. I continued to run my business for a few years while he updated my house, making it a good candidate for selling. Meanwhile, my son Greg was assuming more and more responsibility for the flight school, leaving me free to travel. One of those trips was to New York City, and that's where Don and I were for 9/11.

After 9/11, the airport was never the same—even the areas away from airline operations had to tighten security. We had to screen visitors who wanted to see the airplanes, and we were no longer free to roam the aircraft at other airports. The fun, relaxed atmosphere I had so enjoyed was gone.

Meanwhile, I was approaching the age when airline pilots are required to retire. I remembered giving proficiency checks to aging pilots and watching their skills deteriorate. I didn't want that to happen to me—I preferred to get out at the top of my game.

And so, I decided to retire, and Don and I began making plans for the next chapter of our lives. We wanted to find a place that would be *ours*—not his or mine—and we had a fine time exploring various sites.

Eventually, we decided on Prescott, AZ, and that's where we live now. We are enjoying this interesting town, which is located at 5000 feet altitude and gives us a nice climate. The old west atmosphere and the billing of "Everybody's Hometown" has attracted many other folks who have moved here, and we were all eager to make friends. It's a great place to spend retirement years—or write a book.

My eyes are still drawn to the sky when I hear airplanes, and so are Don's. He traveled often when he was working in sales engineering and made many trips in the company's own planes. He and I enjoy watching aircraft from our front yard as they approach Prescott Airport or practice maneuvers a few thousand feet above us. It's one of the many activities we enjoy; others are entertaining friends and relatives, traveling to places we've seen before and others that are new to us and we love attending the concerts of the Phoenix Symphony Orchestra several times a year here in Prescott.

We love the house we built together - with the help of a few dozen other folks who did the work. It is contemporary, unusual here in Arizona's typically southwestern style structures. Don spends a lot of time landscaping and even created a little grass lawn, also not the norm here. I enjoy hours at my keyboards - my grand piano and my computer. I've just started another new business. There's always something new around the corner.

I'm loving my "retirement years!"

Glossary

a side - a term used when ordering aviation fuel. So if you want to add a total of 40 gallons, you would likely ask for 20 gallons a side. Fuel is stored in the wings.

abeam the numbers - This term is used when a plane is on the downwind leg of the landing pattern, and is flying parallel to the runway. When the pilot looks at the runway and sees the numbers (painted on the runway) 90° to the right or left of the aircraft, that is "abeam the numbers."

active runway - the runway being used currently because of wind conditions or other reasons.

AGL- above ground level, as in 1000 feet agl.

airport bum - a term applied to a person who spends a lot of time hanging out at the airport. It's not a derogatory term.

Airport Facility Directory - a listing of data on record with the FAA on all open-to-the-public airports, seaplane bases, heliports, military facilities, and selected private use airports specifically requested by the Department of Defense (DOD) for which a DOD instrument approach procedure has been published in the US Terminal Procedures Publication, airport sketches, NAVAIDs, communications data, weather data sources, airspace, special notices, VFR waypoints, Airport Diagrams, and operational procedures.

ATP - Airline Transport Pilot - an advanced certificate which requires a minimum of 1500 flight hours and the age of at least 23 years. It is required for airline pilots.

airways and points - routes like highways and points defined by two routes crossing or a navigational fix.

airwork - practice of maneuvers away from the airport, mostly at several thousand feet of altitude.

Approach Control - Many airports have a radar control facility that is associated with the airport. Their controllers are responsible for providing all ATC services within their airspace. Traffic flow is broadly divided into departures, arrivals, and overflights.

ATC - Air Traffic Control - people who issue clearances to airplanes that they are observing either by having them in sight or on a radar screen

attitude - the angular difference measured between an airplane's axis and the line of the Earth's horizon. Pitch attitude is the angle formed by the longitudinal axis, and bank attitude is the angle formed by the lateral axis. Rotation about the airplane's vertical axis (yaw) is termed an attitude relative to the airplane's flightpath, but not relative to the natural horizon. In attitude flying, airplane control is composed of four components: pitch control, bank control, power control, and trim.

attitude flying - visually establishing the airplane's attitude with reference to the natural horizon.

ATIS - Automatic Terminal Information Service - a recording updated each hour or when a significant change is observed. It gives non-control aeronautical information for busier airports.

BAC - Beech Aero Club.

back pressure - pulling back on the yoke, control wheel, or stick, which causes the airplane to climb if it has sufficient power and airspeed, or to stall if it doesn't.

best angle of climb - the speed that gives the aircraft the most altitude gain in a given distance.

best rate of climb - the speed that gives the aircraft the most altitude in the least amount of time.

BFR - biennial flight review - an endorsement from a flight instructor every two years certifying that the pilot has demonstrated the ability to competently perform at the appropriate certificate level both on the ground and in the air.

CAP - Civil Air Patrol - a congressionally chartered, federally supported non-profit corporation serving as the official civilian auxiliary of the US Air Force. It is a volunteer organization including aviation-minded people from all backgrounds, lifestyles, and occupations. It performs three key missions: emergency services including search and rescue as well as disaster relief, aerospace education, and cadet programs for teenagers.

CFI – certified flight instructor

chief flight instructor - an experienced flight instructor who is in charge of the other CFIs. In an FAA approved school, there are specific experience requirements and the person must pass an exam with an FAA inspector in order to qualify.

chocked the plane - put wood or metal blocks in front of and behind at least one wheel.

cleaning up the airplane - in flight, this means retracting the landing gear and putting the flaps up. This usually occurs right after takeoff. After landing, it means retracting the flaps.

combination - some airports have combination locks which prevent unauthorized people from accessing the airplane parking areas.

commercial pilot - a pilot who has met the requirements for the commercial pilot certificate. It is the prerequisite for becoming a hirable commercial pilot and a person can continue training to become a flight instructor, airline transport pilot, etc. It doesn't mean the pilot can automatically fly 747s.

communications radio - a transceiver which can send and receive audio messages.

controlled airport - an airport with a control tower.

coordination - flight with a minimum disturbance of the forces maintaining equilibrium, established by effective control use.

cowling - similar to a hood in a car, it covers the engine compartment of an airplane.

critical engine - in a multiengine airplane, the engine whose failure would result in the most adverse effects on the plane's handling and performance.

Cross 25 and 15 - a clearance to cross runways while taxiing a plane on the airport.

cut off the tail of my shirt - a tradition after a first solo flight: the instructor cuts out a portion of the back of the student pilot's shirt and writes the date and achievement on it.

DG - directional gyro - also known as heading indicator, it's a flight instrument which indicates the aircraft's heading.

dual flight - flight with an instructor, as opposed to solo flight.

FAA designated examiner - A person, appointed by but not employed by the FAA, who is designated to perform specific flight tests.

FARs - Federal Aviation Regulations - can be found at http://www.faa.gov/regulations_policies/faa_regulations/.

FBO - Fixed Base Operator - a commercial business which an airport has given the right to operate on the airport. It can also provide services such as supplying fuel, maintenance, aircraft sales, rentals, and flight training.

flap speed - Most airplanes are placarded to show a maximum speed above which the flaps must not be operated. If operated above this speed, structural failure may occur.

flicker vertigo - an imbalance in brain-cell activity caused by exposure to the low-frequency flickering or flashing of a relatively bright light, such as a rotating beacon, strobe light, or sun seen through a windmilling propeller.

flight at minimum controllable airspeed - minimum flying speed. It is a speed at which any further increase in angle of attack or load factor, or reduction in power, will cause an immediate stall.

flight hours - hours of flight are usually timed by a Hobbs meter. It begins recording time in tenths of hours when the airplane engine is started and stops when the engine is turned off.

flight plan - documents filed by pilots prior to the flight including departure and arrival points, estimated time enroute, alternate airports, type of flight - IFR or VFR etc.

flight school - an organized aviation school where people can learn to fly.

FSS - Flight Service Station - an air traffic facility that provides information and services to pilots before, during, and after flights, but unlike air traffic control (ATC), is not responsible for giving instructions or clearances or providing separation.

fly-ins - organized events involving many airplanes flying to a particular location for the occasion.

Gs - units of the normal pull of gravity experienced on Earth ($32 ft/sec^2$), means that 2 Gs is double that pull, 3 Gs triple, and so on. As a general rule of thumb, the average human can tolerate up to 3.5 Gs (sustained) without losing consciousness, although some individuals could have a tolerance as high as 5 Gs or as low as 2Gs.

gear speed - the maximum speed that allows the landing gear to be lowered.

glide slope - the vertical guidance component of the ILS (Instrument Landing System).

go around – when you discontinue a landing approach by climbing back up to pattern altitude such as 1000 feet agl and repeating the approach.

green arc - a line on an aircraft instrument which is green and indicates the normal range of operation.

ground control - the ATC controller in the Control Tower who is in charge of giving clearances to pilots before they request takeoff and after they leave the runway when they have landed.

ground effect - In fixed-wing aircraft, ground effect is the increased lift and decreased drag that an aircraft's wings generate when they are close to a horizontal surface.

handoff - a change in frequencies for communication.

hangar flying - hanging out at the airport telling and hearing stories about aviation. Enjoyed by people who love flying.

high-density altitude - a condition that occurs when an aircraft is flying in hot, high and humid weather conditions. The air is less dense than usual, which degrades the plane's performance. This can be critical during takeoff and landing.

holding pattern - a delaying technique for when traffic slows down. Airplanes are assigned a "holding fix" such as a VOR or an intersection, an altitude, a direction of turns, and an expected further clearance time.

IFR - Instrument Flight Rules - in effect when the weather is below VFR minimums.

ILS - Instrument Landing System - an internationally normalized system for navigation of aircraft during the final approach for landing. It was accepted as a standard system by the International Civil Aviation Organization in 1947. It is called a precision approach system because it includes a vertical guidance component, the glide slope. Its horizontal guidance component, the localizer, is four times as sensitive as the VOR, which is used for enroute navigation.

instructor - someone who teaches people to fly.

instrument rated pilot - a pilot who is qualified to fly in weather that is below VFR minimums.

intersection - where a runway meets another runway or a taxiway, or where two air routes cross.

LA Center - Los Angeles Air Route Traffic Control Center.

LAX - Los Angeles International Airport.

leaseback - an arrangement for airplane owners to lease their planes back to a flight school or other aviation company. It can reduce the cost of ownership.

left traffic - all left turns in the traffic patterns.

local and departure controllers - a local controller directs traffic from the cab of a control tower where the traffic can be seen. A departure controller controls traffic outside of the airport using a radar screen to observe the aircraft.

localizer - the horizontal guidance component of the ILS (Instrument Landing System).

magnetic course - a course relative to magnetic north.

magneto – engine-driven self-contained unit supplying electrical current without using an external source of power.

magneto check - There are 2 magnetos for each engine in many small airplanes. Before taking off, the pilot performs a runup to a specific power setting. During this runup, the magneto switch is moved from Both to Right to Left and back to Both. The check is to see that the magneto is running smoothly and that the correct reduction of power occurs when just one is operating.

MEA - Minimum Enroute Altitude - the lowest allowed altitude for a segment of enroute instrument flight. It assures navigational signal coverage and obstacle clearance.

minimums - the lowest weather and altitude allowed in order to be able to see the airport following an instrument approach. Otherwise, the pilot must execute a missed approach.

missed approach - the maneuver conducted by a pilot when an instrument approach cannot be completed with a landing for any reason. There is a specific procedure to follow for a missed approach to each runway and each type of instrument approach.

"more right rudder" - a common comment from an instructor to a student because in climbs and other slow flight conditions, right rudder pressure is required to keep the airplane going straight without adding aileron input. Planes are tweaked so that no rudder application is necessary in level cruise flight.

my traffic - aircraft in my vicinity that I need to be aware of.

N number - An aircraft registration is a unique alphanumeric string that identifies a civil aircraft, in similar fashion to a license plate on a car. All aircraft must be registered with a national aviation authority and they must carry a Certificate of Registration at all times when in operation. Most countries also require the aircraft registration to be imprinted on a permanent fireproof plate mounted on the fuselage for the purposes of post-fire/post-crash aircraft accident investigation. Aircraft registered in the US are called N numbers because the registration number here begins with an N.

NDB approach - a non-precision instrument approach that uses an ADF (Automatic Direction Finder) for course guidance.

notam - a notice containing information about the establishment, condition, or change in any aeronautical facility, service, procedures, or hazard. Notices to Airmen are published every 28 days and, if they are written between publications, are read to the pilots during flight briefings for the route and airports they will be encountering.

once around the pattern - a very short flight consisting of a takeoff and maneuvering in the traffic pattern followed by a full stop. It would take about 10 minutes.

over the numbers - above the runway number such as 25, which is painted on the surface.

parallel runways - two or more runways on an airport which go the same direction. If there are two, they are named, for example, 24L and 24R which means that they each have a heading of 240 degrees and one is on the left and the other on the right. If there are three, the third one is called 24C for center. A long skinny airport like LAX may have four: 24L, 24R, 25L and 25R. They appear to all be parallel.

PHAK - Pilot's Handbook of Aeronautical Knowledge - can be viewed or downloaded as a pdf here: http://www.faa.gov/regulations_policies/handbooks_manuals/aviation/pilot_handbook/.

PIC - pilot-in-command.

porpoise - Porpoising may occur if a pilot attempts to force the airplane onto the runway at a higher than normal speed. This allows the nose gear to contact the runway slightly before the main gear does. It can also occur if a pilot lands hard on the main gear, resulting in the airplane pitching forward onto the nose gear. Either way, the airplane responds by pitching up and becoming airborne. The novice pilot typically reacts by applying too much forward elevator pressure, resulting in the nose gear, once again, making hard contact with the runway. The cycle repeats itself, often with more devastating oscillations, sometimes resulting in a damaged nose gear. While an instructor can nurse the plane to a good landing in this situation, a student should initiate a go-around.

position report - a report over a known location which is transmitted by an aircraft to ATC or Flight Service.

practice area - a block of airspace that is suggested for practicing maneuvers. A local tower can tell you where it is. Your flight instructor will show it to you.

precision approach - an instrument approach which has both horizontal and vertical guidance.

preflight - A preflight inspection is performed before each flight. There are checklists for each make and model of aircraft, and these are specific to the year of the airplane.

present position direct, cleared to land - a clearance allowing the pilot to choose a direct path to the runway and a landing clearance.

private pilot certificate - allows a person to fly airplanes for pleasure and to take passengers. He or she cannot charge for flights but can share expenses with the passengers.

radial - course oriented from a VOR navigation facility.

regulations - See FARs above.

roger - an acknowledgement that the transmission has been received. Some pilots incorrectly use it to mean yes.

runup - checks, which are performed at a specific power setting higher than idle, by the pilot before takeoff.

runway names - Runways are named by the their magnetic headings and the last digit is omitted. For example, Runway 24 has a magnetic heading of 240. Each runway has two names, one for each end. The other end of Runway 24 would be Runway 6 because its magnetic heading is 060.

St. Elmo's fire - a corona discharge which lights up aircraft surface areas where maximum static discharge occurs. It is actually plasma rather than fire. The nitrogen and oxygen in the Earth's atmosphere causes St. Elmo's fire to fluoresce with blue or violet light; this is similar to the mechanism that causes neon lights to glow.

Santa Barbara ILS 7 approach - precision approach to Runway 7 at Santa Barbara Airport.

sectional - an aviation map that shows elevations, landmarks, towns, airports, navigational aids, etc., used in VFR (Visual Flight Rules) conditions.

sector - a block of airspace with defined 3D dimensions. Each sector is managed by at least one controller.

short final - when the airplane is lined up with the runway and close to crossing the runway threshold.

slip - an aerodynamic state which results in an airplane moving sideways as well as forward relative to the oncoming airflow. It is caused by not coordinating the ailerons and rudder. It is common for students to enter slips by mistake while turning. However, a slip is a useful tool for increasing the rate of descent when approaching to land. Commonly used with airplanes without flaps.

short field takeoff and landing - techniques for taking off and landing on runways that are short and/or have obstacles at the ends.

soft field takeoff and landing - techniques for taking off and landing on runways that are soft because of snow, mud, grass, etc.

special VFR clearance - when the weather is below VFR minimums, a pilot may request a clearance to operate, usually departing or arriving at an airport, when flight visibility is at least one statute mile and the airplane can remain clear of clouds.

squawk - a four digit number dialed in and transmitted by an aircraft transponder.

squawks - maintenance problems that require repair or attention.

stage checks - oral and flight tests given by the Chief Flight Instructor during a course such as private, IFR, etc.

stall - Contrary to common belief, a stall in an airplane isn't due to the engine stopping. It actually occurs when the angle of attack of the wing increases beyond a point where the lift decreases. At the critical angle of attack, the airplane loses its lift (stall), which in most small airplanes causes the plane to pitch down, thereby building up airspeed which takes the airplane out of the stalled condition.

stall warning - FAA certification rules for airplanes require that the airplane provides pilots with unmistakable warnings of an impending stall. In a small airplane, it is usually buffeting or shaking.

This is most often preceded by an aural warning horn and sometimes a light.

steep turns - turns which have a bank angle of 45 to 60°. They are taught and practiced in the private and commercial pilot courses. Because they require quite a bit of back pressure to compensate for the loss of lift due to the bank angle, it is important for the pilot to be able to do them correctly if one is ever required. A level 60° bank pulls 2Gs.

three times around the patch - flying the traffic pattern three times, including 2 touch and goes and a full stop; the standard for a first solo.

tail numbers - An aircraft registration is a unique alphanumeric string that identifies a civil aircraft, in similar fashion to a license plate on a car. Because airplanes typically display their registration numbers on the aft fuselage just forward of the tail, or in earlier times more often on the tail itself, the registration is often referred to as the "tail number."

threw the yoke over - an option for Beechcraft Bonanzas and Barons is a throw over yoke. It is an easily installed single yoke that can be "thrown over" from the left front seat to the right and vice versa. It is nice when you have someone in the right seat who is not interested in flying and wants more room.

tiedown - Since airplanes are built to fly, the lighter ones need to be tied down when they are parked so they don't move without human assistance. They are usually secured with ropes or chains.

touch and goes - performing circuits of the traffic pattern with a landing followed immediately by another takeoff.

trimming - setting up the controls of an airplane so that it can fly without the pilot having to apply pressure to maintain the desired attitude.

true course - the resulting track over the ground which is achieved by correcting for wind, measured in true rather than magnetic degrees.

TRSA - Terminal Radar Service Area - an area where pilots could receive radar service, which provides separation between all IFR operations and participating VFR aircraft.

twin - an aircraft with two engines.

uncontrolled airport - an airport without a control tower.

unicom - stands for Universal Communications - an air-ground communication facility operated by a non- air traffic control private agency to provide advisory service such as weather information, wind direction, the runway in use, and reported traffic at uncontrolled airports.

unusual attitudes - any unanticipated situation where an aircraft is placed into a position where pitch exceeds 25° nose up or 10° nose down, yaw is greater than 45, and airspeed is unsuitable for the condition. Recovery from these situations is included in pilot training.

variation - Correct name is magnetic variation, which is the difference between true north and magnetic north. It varies with location.

VASI - visual slope indicator. The VASI is a system of lights arranged so as to provide visual descent guidance information during the approach to a runway.

vector - a magnetic heading given to an aircraft from Air Traffic Control.

vectored a long ways before intercepting the final approach course - given directions of which heading to fly before being cleared to intercept the navigation signal that would bring you straight in to the runway. It is a delaying tactic to manage spacing.

VFR - Visual Flight Rules - weather conditions that allow a pilot to operate by reference to objects outside the cockpit. There are specific requirements for minimum visibility and distance from clouds.

Vmc - minimum controllable speed with the critical engine inoperative in a multiengine aircraft.

VOR - very high frequency omnidirectional radio range. A short range radio navigation system for aircraft. It is the standard air navigational system worldwide, used by both commercial and general aviation.

walk around - a preflight inspection of an aircraft.

x-c - abbreviation for cross country.

Made in the USA
San Bernardino, CA
25 March 2020

66335624R00140